Commit To Quality

Patrick L. Townsend
with Joan E. Gebhardt

A Wiley Press Book

JOHN WILEY & SONS, INC.

New York • Chichester • Brisbane • Toronto • Singapore

Publisher: Stephen Kippur
Editor: Elizabeth G. Perry
Managing Editor: Katherine Schowalter
Editing, Design, and Production: Publication Services

Wiley Press books can be used as premiums to promote products or services, for training, or in mail-order catalogs. For information on quantity discounts, please write to the Special Sales Department, John Wiley & Sons, Inc.

Copyright © 1986 by Patrick L. Townsend

All rights reserved. Published simultaneously in Canada.

Reproduction or translation of any part of this work beyond that permitted by Section 107 or 108 of the 1976 United States Copyright Act without the permission of the copyright owner is unlawful. Requests for permission or further information should be addressed to the Permissions Department, John Wiley & Sons, Inc.

Library of Congress Cataloging in Publication Data:

Townsend, Patrick L.
  Commit to quality.

  Includes index.
  1. Quality assurance. 2. Quality circles. 3. Value analysis (Cost control) I. Gebhardt, Joan E. II. Title.
HD66.T65   1986   658.5'62   85-29639
ISBN 0-471-83953-1

Printed in the United States of America

86 87 10 9 8 7 6 5 4 3 2

For Michael and Brady

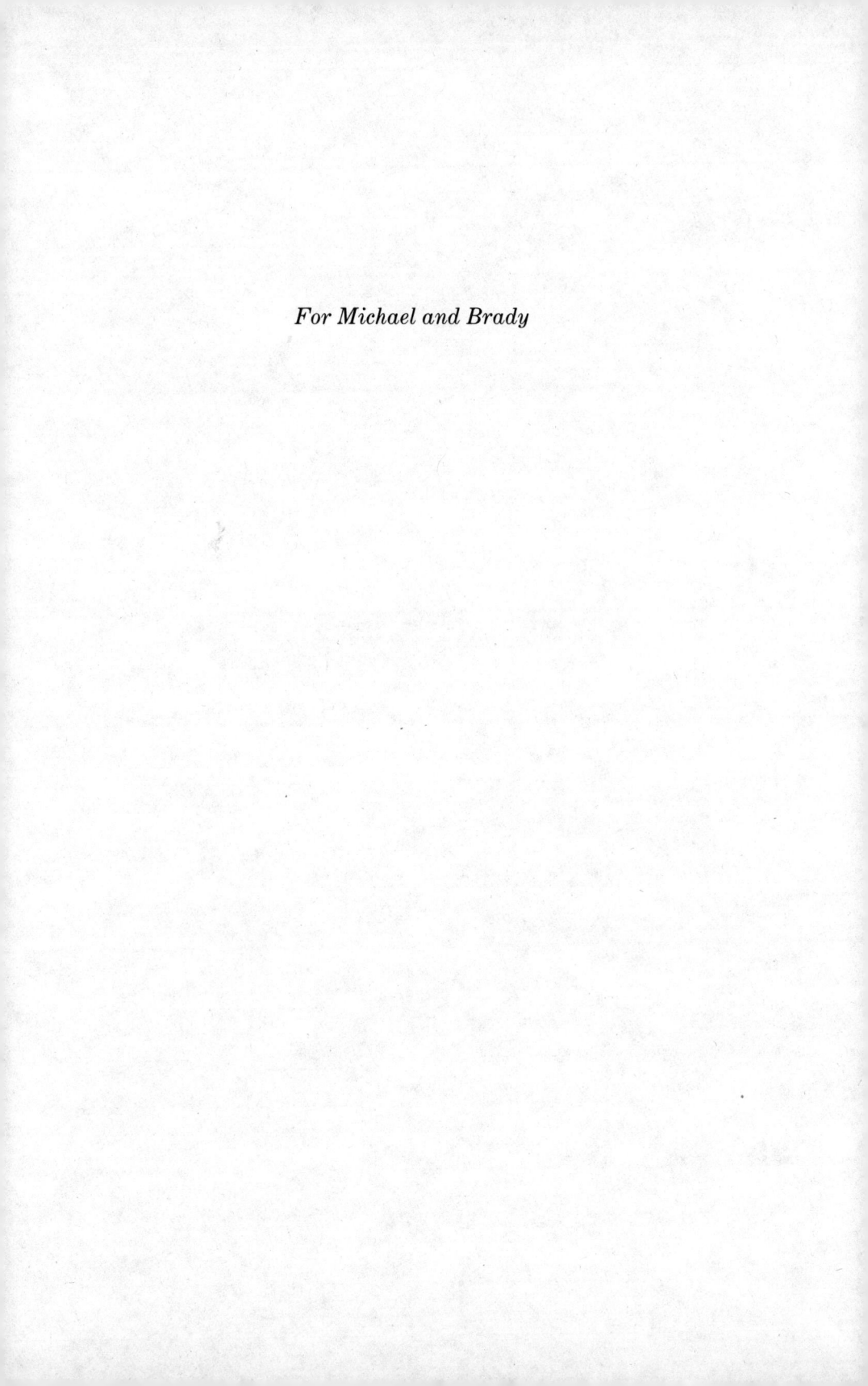

Acknowledgments

While acknowledging my obvious debt to such renowned figures as Tom Peters, Phil Crosby, and Dr. Deming, I owe an even greater debt of gratitude to the employees of The Paul Revere Insurance Companies of Worcester, Massachusetts, who have validated this process through their actions. I must thank The Paul Revere for taking a chance on a former Marine with a funny-looking résumé and then stretching their odds even further by giving me so much control over the implementation of the Quality Has Value process. Without the support of Aubrey K. Reid (President), Bill Pearson (Co-chairman of the Quality Steering Committee and Vice-President of Human Resources), Chuck Soule (Co-chairman of the Quality Steering Committee and Vice-President of Operations), and Al Materas (my first boss at The Paul Revere), success would not have been possible. Nor would it have been possible without the patience, enthusiasm, and technical knowledge of the members of Quality Team Central—Ray Perkins, Selma White, Cheryl Alderman, Rick Perez, and Jill Langowski—or the help and skill of Bill Domings (Director—Value Analysis).

My background prior to joining The Paul Revere Insurance Companies in the fall of 1983 was twenty years in the Marine Corps. I submit that military leadership theory is a rich, though overlooked, lode available for mining. It represents a methodology worked out over thousands of years in an arena in which the penalty for error is quick and severe. I learned about leadership from men who were my commanders—Dan

Blaul and Robert C. "Bud" McFarlane (my first commanding officers), Glenn Skulborstad (Army), Peter J. Mulroney, Larry Dorsa, Bob Keller, and Paul Lessard (Marine colonels), and Jack Wheeler (Navy). I learned also from friends such as Skip Bartlett, Frank Capin, Don Rosenberg, and Mike Romero.

Thanks also to John Greenwood of the *Marine Corps Gazette* and Sid McKeen of the *Worcester Evening Gazette* for encouraging my early efforts.

Joan Gebhardt, my collaborator, is invaluable. Without her, I would still be circulating a tentative proposal to various publishers.

Contents

Foreword by Tom Peters	ix
Preface	xv
1. Getting Started	1
Setting the Stage	2
Defining the Dual Nature of Quality	3
Relating Quality and Productivity	6
The Indispensable Participant	8
Establishing a Committee	12
Setting the Parameters	13
Outlining the Plan	15
2. Quality Is Everybody's Business	19
Identifying the Customer	21
Publicizing the Effort	23
Getting Outside Help	25
Refining the Details	26
"Ready, Fire, Aim"	31
3. Value Analysis	33
Using a Consultant	34
Organizing a Workshop	36
Arriving at an Essential Purpose	39
Diagramming and Rating Functions	40
Considering Options	44
Implementing Changes	46
4. Quality Teams: An Improvement on Quality Circles	51
Involving Everyone in Quality	55
Training Team Leaders	57
Establishing Teams	60
Achieving Results	64

	Quality Teams—Beyond Quality Circles	66
	Making a Commitment	73
5.	**Virtue Is Not Necessarily Its Own Reward**	**77**
	Understanding Maslow's Theory	78
	Applying the Principles	81
	Setting the Standards	84
	Rewarding Success	87
	Adding Variety	90
	Celebrating: Don't Forget to Party	94
	Launching a Second Year	98
6.	**Change in Corporate Culture**	**101**
	Quality Ideas	101
	Training	108
	Publications	116
	Feedback	119
	Value Analysis	123
7.	**Quality Has Value: The Second Year**	**125**
	Determining the Cost of Quality	125
	Providing a Focus	128
	Modifying Quality Has Value—Team Leaders	131
	Beginning Again	134
8.	**Listening Down—And Out**	**141**
	Recognizing a Pattern	142
	Overcoming Management Resistance	145
	Establishing Mutual Trust	148
	Nurturing New Habits	151
	Extending Listening Down to the Field	155
	Maximizing Benefits	157
9.	**Adopting Theory and Adapting Practice**	**161**
Appendix: A Blueprint for Quality		**171**
	Commitment—The Unit Boss	171
	Commitment—The Next Level of Management	171
	The Committee	172
	Definitions and Goals	173
	The Plan	173
	Training	176
	Recognition, Gratitude, and Celebration	178
	Communications	178
	Chief Mechanic	178
References		**181**
Index		**185**

Foreword

"A decision to institute a Quality Team process is, if you will, a decision to allow a revolution.... The outpouring of ideas was staggering."

The quality pins were redesigned [for 1985], but not because the 1984 design was unsatisfactory or because it was believed that people enjoyed amassing a collection of lapel pins. Rather, the change was precipitated because many of the female employees did not like sticking the pseudo-tie tack through their garments. As a result, more than a few had missed a free lunch because they had chosen not to wear their pins on the day when their name had been picked. The 1985 pins were designed to come in two styles—tie tack with the push-through post and clutch, and charm with a small loop for hanging from a necklace or bracelet. The percentage of female employees wearing their Quality Pins immediately rose, resulting in that many more reminders to everyone about Quality...and more free lunches.

Pat Townsend has written a superb book about the Quality Has Value process instituted at The Paul Revere, an insurance company that is a subsidiary of Textron, Inc. As the opening quotes suggest, it at once deals with the most abstract philosophical ideas (allow a revolution) and the most mundane attributes of execution (two types of pins, to be more responsive to women in the organization).

There are at least two important reasons to read Townsend's book. First, it is, to my knowledge, the first book on the quality process to deal exclusively with a service business. And, let there be no mistake, the American economy is, now, a service economy. Second, Townsend spares no detail in laying out the process. Many have written about quality circle programs and the like (Townsend goes way out of his way to discriminate between The Paul Revere process and the standard quality circle process), but few have spelled it out on a minute-by-minute basis over a two-year period. We have the rare opportunity to learn from every one of his and Paul Revere's mistakes, and to share their triumphs—from the design of lapel pins to the selection of outside consultants (and the decision as to when to let them go).

Let me begin with the two different levels of abstraction. Pat does a fine job of describing the philosophy of the Quality Team process. It begins, not surprisingly, with top management commitment. Most, for instance Phil Crosby, are insistent in beginning with a nod to top management involvement. Townsend puts chapter and verse around the idea. That is: top management at The Paul Revere first promised that no one would be laid off as a result of a Quality Team idea that might have reduced staffing as a consequence. Moreover, The Paul Revere senior management encouraged substantial on-the-job time for team training and team problem solving. They also devoted a substantial amount of time to celebrating the successes of teams.

Pat describes the philosophic change in graphic detail: "As the first year progressed at The Paul Revere, the word 'Quality' became a velvet club. Previously, if a person walked into someone's office and said, 'I've got an idea I'd like to talk about...', they stood a fair chance of being scheduled sometime near the end of the decade. Now, however, if the opening line is, 'I've got a Quality idea and my team would like some information...', the response is almost always, 'Let's talk about it. What do you need?'" He illustrates the process with a concrete example that brought it all home to me:

> "So 'small' ideas were allowed, even encouraged, so long as it could be shown that the idea had been implemented and that it had a positive impact on the Quality of the unit.... Team

leaders were urged to begin with a few small ideas to build momentum. Many teams received credit for things as simple, and as small, as moving a file cabinet ten feet closer to the one person who has frequent use of it. A Quality idea? Technically, perhaps not—but the inconvenient location of that cabinet had most likely been a matter of irritation fifteen times a day for the person who had to walk the extra dozen or so steps. Could it have been moved prior to the Quality Has Value process? Perhaps in theory it could have been, but the person being inconvenienced did not believe it, or did not want to go through the hassle of asking permission through however many layers of management that it would have taken."

Opening up the organization is what the Townsend message is all about. And the way to do it is, indeed, to start small. He stresses that again and again.

At the highest level of abstraction, Pat ties The Paul Revere process to the Maslow hierarchy of needs, starting with survival and moving on to self actualization. In this vein, an entire chapter speaks to the issue of "listening down;" that is, managers at all levels listening to their people.

The most important aspect of the book for me was the alpha to omega treatment of the implementation of the quality process. Townsend devotes substantial space to distinguishing between The Paul Revere process (focusing on the term Quality Team) and the standard quality circle approach. The principal difference, he asserts, is the *non-volunteer* aspect of The Paul Revere program. Townsend suggests that a typical quality circle process involves only a small percentage of people at any facility. The Paul Revere process, which was initially employed with the 1,200 people at corporate headquarters, involved *everyone*! All, from the president to the newest hired receptionist, were mandated into the process. Townsend believes this to be the greatest distinction between the Paul Revere process (which was an exceptional success) and the standard quality circle program as introduced at most companies. He has a good point.

From a structural standpoint, he picks up on a vital notion that has been in the wind for years. He speaks of a "shadow organization." That is, the process of forming Quality Teams and appointing Quality Team Leaders became an overlay on the overall Paul Revere organization. The "Quality Team Leader" position, for instance, became an alternative route to promotability (or at least visibility) within the organization.

Details of every aspect of program execution are rife throughout the book. For example, the Quality Team Tracking Program, wholly computer-based, is described in depth. It eliminated paperwork involved in the implementation of a massive program. But at the same time, it allowed Paul Revere people to be in exact touch, on a team-by-team and day-by-day basis, with what was transpiring.

In the past several years I have been impressed with two quality programs in particular: one at Milliken Co. (the giant Spartanburg, South Carolina-based textile company) and the one Pat describes at The Paul Revere. Though Townsend spends a large share of his time on issues such as non-volunteerism, the most common thread that I find between the Milliken program and his is the attention to 1,001 details which serve to build momentum over the course of time.

I don't know how to best direct the reader's attention to this attribute of the book. I want to say, "Read it, re-read it, re-read it again." That is, read it for the philosophy (volunteer versus non-volunteer, Quality Team versus quality circle), but above all read it for the *vast* array of small ideas.

At the heart of the matter is, among other things, the celebration process. Bronze, Silver, and Gold medals abound. By now, even a Septuple Gold has been awarded. It's the fine-grained details of awarding—e.g., lower levels of senior management give awards to the newly-Bronzed teams, and the company president (with photographer in tow) gives awards to the newly-minted Gold teams. It's living with Pat through a program that was lagging at one point; in order to improve visibility, the Lunch For A Pin process was established. That is, a dozen or so names were drawn from a hat; if any of those people were wearing their quality pins at the time, they would be awarded a free lunch. To top it off, at the end of the year Paul Revere engaged in a Quality Celebration, including everything from a half-day off to appropriately embossed balloons for all.

Most quality programs fail to reach their potential for one of two reasons. They have the spirit, but fail to match it with attention to executional details, especially the momentum-building details which are required as time rolls by and energy naturally dissipates. Or, conversely, they have the techniques down to a tee (doubtless taught to them by an overly expensive outside consultant), but the spirit is not there—that is, the average person doesn't feel that the door has been truly opened in any way, shape or form. It is the rare analysis—i.e., this one—which covers both sides of the issue with equal rigor.

Moreover, as noted, this is to my knowledge the *sole* analysis which deals specifically and exclusively with a service industry. Certainly, there is wholesale transferability to non-service settings. On the other hand, most of us are not prone to generalize, and tend to downgrade analyses that don't come from our arena. For those who think that the quality programs that we read about at Ford et al. won't work in the service environment, this book is the long-awaited answer.

Read it for its philosophy, read it for its practicality, and then get on with it. The issues that Townsend raises are vital. The practical progress in a tough environment that he can demonstrate makes a compelling case.

Tom Peters

Preface

Commit to Quality brings something new to the growing collection of management books—a clear blueprint for achieving quality. The procedures described and the theory supporting them enable readers to mold practices to their own needs, whether the setting is service or manufacturing industries, academia, or community groups.

A unique amalgam of participative management, quality teams, value analysis, and suggestions systems, leavened and made immediate with yankee common sense and ingenuity, the Quality Has Value Process is based on hands-on experience. An already profitable paper-and-ideas company, The Paul Revere Insurance Companies, used these methods both to better its competitive position and to build the morale of its employees.

The results are spectacular, a quantum leap forward from other methods currently used. In 1984, the first year of Quality Has Value, combining value analysis recommendations and the use of over 4,110 ideas contributed by 1,200 employees, the company was able to realize a saving of over $8.5 million on an annualized basis. The same process has had even more dramatic results in 1985. This success substantiates the rather daring idea that quality as a vitalizing force not only applies to manufacturing firms but can serve equally well in a paper-and-ideas (service) company.

Quality Has Value is a successful combination of two ideas that many management observers have said could not possibly coexist: Quality Teams and Value Analysis. Quality teams are not quality circles; the differences between the two concepts are important ones; indeed, they warrant a whole chapter in this book.

Commit to Quality shows how The Paul Revere instituted a quality process that involved everyone from the company president to the newest person hired—and how others can do the same. It describes the procedures used by The Paul Revere when the process was begun and examines the component parts of the plan in detail in succeeding chapters: the formation of Value Analysis workshops and Quality Teams; the training of leaders; the program of recognition, gratitude, and celebration; techniques of enlisting the wholehearted cooperation of middle management (in our experience, the segment of the company that found it most difficult to become involved in the process); how to secure the cooperation of every employee; and the far-reaching results and implications of a move toward quality.

The description of the process at The Paul Revere details not only how the plan works but also why. Readers might find the why more significant than the how, since the how is flexible—the theory can be adopted and the practice adapted without weakening the process or the rationale behind it.

It is possible that a reader will gather from this book that all the features of the Quality Has Value process at The Paul Revere came into maturity simultaneously. This is true—it happened that way, however, only after a period of preparation that lasted nearly a year. This book can dramatically reduce that preparation time. It can be used to set goals, decide on procedures, define a solid training program, and establish a nurturing, supportive atmosphere. The chapters that describe the remarkable success of the Quality Has Value process can be a rich source of ideas for adoption and adaptation.

By the end of the first year, the number of completed ideas for a Quality Team was more than nine times that reported for a quality circle in Japan. The rate of implementation of ideas per employee was more than 350 times that reported as the national average by the National Association of Suggestion Systems. The over 16,000 ideas submitted in the first two years attest to the fact that the distinctive procedures and unique definitions that evolved are particularly well suited to today's employees who want to have more control over their work environment and, at the same time, are willing to share their vast first-hand knowledge of the work they do. The process described in *Commit to Quality* gives them that opportunity.

Unlike the common "Don't look for any real results for the first year or so" warning that comes with most quality circle packages, the process provided returns the first week it was formally launched. That is the short-term gain. The long-term gain is nothing less than a change in corporate culture, that is, that set of rules and assumptions, written and unwritten, that guide the day-to-day actions of just about everyone in the organization. As the company president said in his initial letter to all employees, this is not a "quick fix program." It is one that will be permanent, with goals established as we move ahead, to meet changing conditions and changing demands. And move ahead we shall, with the hope that, through this book, others will be inspired to do so as well.

Patrick L. Townsend

1

Getting Started

"Quality is job one." "The quality goes in before the name goes on." "Quality that never goes out of style." American advertisers tout quality as the Holy Grail of modern America—the universal good sought by all. Once an assumed attribute of American products, quality now more often becomes the operative factor in a decision to buy.

The industry that proclaims quality offers an implied contract between itself and the customer—a promise of superior performance, durability, satisfaction, and a good maintenance record. The company that advertises quality, however, had better deliver if it wants to keep those profits. A disappointed customer does not buy twice. Dr. W. Edwards Deming, the man who introduced Japanese manufacturers to statistical quality control as the centerpiece of an all-encompassing quality process, and who rightfully receives much of the credit for the astounding Japanese quality revolution, says, "Who can put a price on a satisfied customer, and who can figure the cost of a dissatisfied customer?"

Quality reached the pinnacle of official American acceptance and visibility in 1984 when President Ronald Reagan designated October as "Quality Month," which he said he hoped would signal "to the American people the importance of top quality in all we do." The President explained, "Our forefathers were fine craftsmen; they were committed to quality and to teamwork. They taught us that teams of skilled workers, motivated and with the opportunity to contribute, can turn out products of the highest excellence. It is up to us to recommit ourselves to that spirit today."

The importance of quality cannot be overstated. William R. Thurston, president and CEO of the high-tech company GenRad Inc., asserted in an article titled "Quality Is Between the Customer's Ears" that "any company that doesn't solve its quality issues over the next 10 years will be out of business." Donald Ephlin, Vice President of the United Auto Workers, puts it succinctly: "Quality is job security today.... There's no sense in being competitive in cost if you're not competitive in quality."

The word "quality" is commonly associated with manufacturing applications. "Quality control" is achieved in a manufacturing setting by such disciplines as precise measurements, statistical tracking of variations from standards, and mechanical operations following a preset plan. Measuring devices and statistical control charts, however, are of little use when dealing with a service or information industry.

A seemingly endless stream of insurance policies, all precisely the same size, all perfectly proofread, all with smudge-proof ink, are irrelevant to the quality of the financial protection they represent. Producing an object that is physically perfect does not solve the problems of quality for a paper-and-ideas industry. Convenience, promptness, courtesy, reliability, and other "soft" measurements more often serve as criteria for determining a quality service company.

The good news is that not only is it possible to achieve quality in a service industry, it is also possible to measure it. And, since the conservative estimate is that by the year 2000, 80 percent of American workers will be employed in service industries, an approach that is proven to work in such a setting is of critical importance.

Setting the Stage

Between January and December of 1984, The Paul Revere Insurance Companies, headquartered in Worcester, Massachusetts, instituted a process called "Quality Has Value" (QHV). As an insurance company, The Paul Revere represents a hybrid of the service and manufacturing worlds, and the lessons learned can be applied to both. Unlike a "pure" service industry such as a hotel, an insurance company does produce a product with definable, tangible worth. Yet that product's physical perfection is incidental. The thought and research that goes into the policy gives the paper and ink its value. Insurance companies are a microcosm of American business. They include a combination of high-tech and low-tech, low-cost individual sales and high finance, intense competition and mundane work.

The Paul Revere, a consistent money-maker, nevertheless had lost the number one position in its bread-and-butter product, disability insurance. Growth, while steady, was slow. Everyone was aware that something had to happen.

That something was to set quality as a goal for the company. It should be emphasized that the process that resulted was not an attempt to save a company from impending bankruptcy, rather, it was a demonstration of creative thinking on the part of management. While it is feasible to use quality as Chrysler did to ward off disaster, companies that see an effort to improve quality as something to turn to only in dire circumstances are missing a tremendous opportunity. An emphasis on quality is available to any corporation as a way of making a larger profit.

Pursuing quality, however, must begin with a useable definition. To proceed without a firm, mutually agreeable definition would be like setting off for Oz with each person following a different-colored brick road. The chances of everyone getting to the same place, much less getting there at the same time, would diminish with each passing day.

Defining the Dual Nature of Quality

Two examples of quality illustrate common uses of the word. Ford's slogan, "Quality is job one," points to an attempt to convince the buying public that it considers quality its top priority and that nothing will come off the assembly line that does not measure up to Ford's specifications. Every car will be the same as all the others.

On the other hand, Willis Reed was known as a "quality ballplayer." Fans used the word somewhat differently. They agreed that Reed embodied everything they expected—and wanted—in a major star. He had the requisite statistics (i.e., number of points and rebounds), but he also provided inspiration and courage. His willingness to sacrifice for the team, to play with pain (witness the 1970 championship game against the Los Angeles Lakers), and his obviously gentle, and gentlemanly, demeanor set him above others with similar, or even better, statistics. Enter subjectivity.

Albeit overlapping, two distinct types of quality emerge—Quality in Fact and Quality in Perception. The provider of goods or services who through dint of hard work and capital expenditures performs up to its own specifications achieves Quality in Fact. Traditional definitions of productivity center on the same concept. It is also the definition used by Phil Crosby in *Quality Is Free*. Crosby says that quality is "conformance to specifications," an explanation that implies that the only specifications that matter are those defined by the manufacturer. Dr. J. M. Juran's definition, "fitness for use" also leaves many questions not only unanswered but unasked. Juran and Crosby both leave the defining of quality solely within the province of the producer. Such a definition falls short of being truly useful in the pursuit of quality.

The other quality type is Quality in Perception—the subjective quality as the customer sees it. A product or service achieves Quality in Perception when it meets the customer's expectations. It means being *believed* to be as good as, or better than, the customer expects.

For sustained success, close attention must be paid to both aspects of quality. To demonstrate the point and the interrelationship of the two aspects of quality, consider feeding supper to an average child. Tonight the family chef has prepared spinach casserole. Nothing but the finest ingredients have been used, with the recipe followed meticulously. The spinach casserole has, indeed, attained Quality in Fact and is ready to go to the table, or marketplace.

A loud "yuck" serves as a "soft" but accurate measure of the Quality in Perception of the spinach casserole in the eyes of the customer, little Reginald.

The producer's options are:
1. Threaten Reggie's life if he doesn't eat it—a choice not frequently available in normal business transactions.
2. Convince Reginald, through a fact-based, statistics-enhanced, celebrity-endorsed lecture, of the great worth of the spinach casserole so that he practically begs to be allowed to have some.
3. Modify the dish—by the addition of cheese or ice cream or whatever—until the Quality in Fact and the Quality in Perception find some common ground.
4. Feed the dish to the dog, ask young Reginald what he would like for supper, and fix it well—thus matching the Quality in Fact to the predefined Quality in Perception expectations.

If a manufacturer, or provider of services, does things exactly as it intends to, its output will be a quality product; it fulfills the requirements necessary to be labeled "Quality in Fact." If it is not perceived as quality, that is, its intended customer believes it to fall short of his or her expectations, no sale will occur. To ignore the implications of the dual nature of quality is to court disaster. The relationship between the two is multiplicative, not additive; a zero for either reduces the total to zero. The possibility of bankruptcy with a complete inventory of quality products does exist.

A company can spend months, or perhaps years, designing a new product, only to find that no one cares. The Coca-Cola Company and "New Coke" are a recent example. The object offered met exactly the specifications of its proud parent; however, due to lack of advertising or some misjudgment in the needs analysis phase of the product design, not enough of the ultimate judges were willing to trade their money for it.

The Sara Lee case offers another interesting example of how sales can be crippled when you have Quality in Fact but not Quality in Perception. When Sara Lee offered a top-quality frozen cheesecake at a low price, sales were poor. The public felt that such a low-priced product could not be of high quality. Then the company raised the price of the cheesecake, and sales boomed. By raising the price, Sara Lee raised the customer's expectations, which fortunately they met.

Legions of starving, highly talented artists attest to the need for customer perception of quality if there is to be a sale. Thurston's definition of quality is representative of how more and more relative weight is being given to Quality in Perception: "Quality is what the customer perceives when he feels the product meets his needs and lives up to his expectations."

This is especially true for companies selling ideas or services. It will be extremely difficult for such a company to win back customers lost because they perceive the company to have low standards. Buyers cannot run their hands over an idea, and they are less likely to take a company's word for any improvement without tangible products with hard statistics to back corporate assertions.

Grasping the two aspects of quality is readily possible for those with a view of the big picture, that is, those at the top of the corporate ladder and, perhaps, for the salespeople who must come face to face with the people who actually put out money for the product in question.

But what of the vast majority of the employees of the producing company? Is it necessary for them to understand this concept? Yes. Their efforts determine if the product is to meet the Quality in Fact measurements; their impact on Quality in Perception is not as self-evident, but it is overwhelming. All employees must have an understanding of the concept of quality if quality is to be used as a goal.

Relating Quality and Productivity

The dual-faceted definition of quality that encompasses fact and perception illuminates the difference between quality and productivity. Productivity and Quality in Fact overlap considerably. Increases in Quality in Fact can lead directly to increases in productivity. Emphasis on Quality in Fact in manufacturing operations, through the use of statistical quality control can, in the words of Ken Kivenko, President of Bendix Aviation Electric Ltd., lead to the conversion of the "'hidden factory' that produces scrap, rework, repairs, sorting and customer complaints to productive use." Further in his article "Quality & Productivity: An Inseparable Team," Kivenko points out that "From 15 percent to 49 percent of the manufacturer's cost of almost any American product is for waste embedded in it." No wonder he warns that "too great a deterioration of quality may lead to economic catastrophe."

But productivity is not quality. Quality incorporates productivity. One difference was defined by a second vice-president at The Paul Revere Insurance Companies when she said, "Productivity means counting the beans. Quality means making sure the bean plants grow well."

Warde Wheaton, Executive Vice President of the Honeywell Aerospace and Defense Group, recognizes the difference. He was quoted in an American Productivity Center report as saying,

> ...we feel productivity can best be increased through improvement in our quality of work. When the quality of work output from each individual improves, the next person in the process receives a product or service meeting their requirements, thereby reducing costly rework. People want to do better, and will, provided they are given the opportunity to participate, are properly motivated and given the adequate training and tools to be competent.

Another, more subtle, difference between productivity and quality is important to companies deciding to launch a drive to improve themselves. In the minds of many American workers, an effort to improve productivity will lead to fewer jobs, and there is no denying that this could indeed be so. After all, the goal of increased productivity is to do the same thing using fewer assets—and people are assets. A quality process should not be identified with this idea. A quality process must be presented—to union as well as nonunion work forces—as one that means doing the current work better with the same work force. And if the product, service, or information being offered in the marketplace is changed for the better, sales will improve. That means more jobs and job security.

Productivity is not the issue; quality is. A survey of U.S. consumers in 1981 by the American Society for Quality Control indicated that 49.9 percent of those polled felt that the quality of American goods had dropped since 1976, even though American workers retain their place as the most productive in the world. Each worker produced an average of $26,615 worth of finished goods in 1982. That led the second-place Japanese by 31 percent—despite the fact that the average Japanese worker spent twenty-six more days on the job than his American counterpart.

There is a need to change this perception. With competition intensifying and the entire world becoming an international marketplace, Deming says, "We in America will have to be more protectionist or more competitive. The choice is very simple. If we are to become more competitive, then we have to begin with our quality."

The Indispensable Participant

The first, and critical, requirement for improving quality is that the manager of the unit involved makes a deep commitment to the process and its goals and becomes personally active in the pursuit of those goals. Charles Harwood, President of Signetics Corporation, cautions that upper management must be aware of the "'manager's apparent-interest index' which says, in effect, 'people watch your feet, not your lips.' If the boss does a lot of preaching but doesn't invest a lot of hours of effort himself, people see through it."

Ideally, this boss would be the President or CEO of the entire organization. Dr. Deming began his campaign in Japan by insisting that the company leaders be involved in the effort. "Otherwise," he said, "you will go on like the Americans and make the same mistakes as they are making."

A pioneer effort at The Paul Revere in 1981 illustrates that one dedicated, determined person within a corporate structure can make a significant impact on the quality of the segment for which he or she is responsible. Even in an inhospitable corporate environment, one person can make a difference. It requires creativity, concern, and self-confidence.

The first formal quality effort at The Paul Revere was more what Tom Peters calls a skunkworks—a quasi-revolutionary, slightly smelly, bootleg operation run in just one department of a company. The head of one department at The Paul Revere had previously owned his own business; so when he took over a department that had fallen on hard times, evidenced by slipping productivity and falling morale, he decided to treat it as a separate, small business with no particular regard for the "company way." He began the Employee Achievement Award Program. The first paragraph of the initiating announcement read:

> Beginning on March 1st our Department will have its *own* program (not a Company-sponsored program) to recognize and reward those people putting out 'superior effort'—as defined later. The *purpose* of the program is *twofold*—to single out and reward those people already performing at high levels and to motivate everyone to strive for the same standards of excellence.

The remainder of the bulletin was a question-and-answer format beginning:

> Q: How will the program work?
> A: Basically, we plan to select a monthly winner from each of three units—Pensions (plus three secretaries), Financial Administration plus Proposal Unit, and Administration Services. The three monthly winners will receive a prize and also become eligible for a quarterly award—a winner and a runner-up. Of course, it could work out that a unit does not have a winner in a given month, but we hope that isn't true. There would be up to nine people eligible for the quarterly award.

The judging was to be based on eight points: volume, quality, improvement, time service, attendance, tardiness, extras, and attitude. Quality was described: "This is tougher, but through feedback from the Field, from clients, and from within it's not hard to get a handle on who is doing high quality, accurate work."

Monthly award winners were to "be nominated by their own unit members up through the chain to their unit head." As many as three nominations from each of the three units would then go to a selection committee that would include the previous month's and quarter's winners. The awards ranged from free lunches in the cafeteria for monthly winners to a twenty-five-dollar certificate at a very posh restaurant for the quarterly winner. What was not mentioned was that all prizes were being paid for by the department head.

The closing question and answer read:

Q: Finally, please repeat why we're doing this?
A: That's a good question. We are genuinely concerned with recognizing personal achievement in the form of the type of "superior effort," which we tried to describe earlier. We also would like to stimulate or promote the kind of attitude throughout the department that makes that kind of effort possible by everyone. We are *not* merely reacting to the backlogs and difficult situation we find ourselves in currently. That situation is a *temporary* one and the program we are describing is intended to be an ongoing one. Furthermore, we hope that you all will be winners and we think that you can be.

The employees of the department reacted with enthusiasm and responsibility. It was not unheard of for a unit to withhold nominations for a particular month if they felt that they had not carried their share of the load that month.

The program worked wonderfully for about a year, while other department heads made cautious inquiries as to what was in the works. But nobody imitated it. This was partially because, while the company President did not disallow it, neither did he officially endorse it. When the man who had begun it was promoted away from the department, the program quickly withered and died. Corporate backing was missing.

In early 1983, three separate thinking processes, none consciously tied to the earlier single-department effort, began to emerge. This proved to be the foundation for the commitment that The Paul Revere top management eventually made.

The Operations Division Vice-President began to talk up the idea of quality and offered the opinion that this was a possible way to propel the company back to the top. The Chairman of the Board of AVCO, then the parent company of The Paul Revere, prepared a directive to all AVCO companies, instructing them to institute quality efforts. (AVCO was purchased by Textron, Inc. in December 1984.) The directive is quoted here in full because it contains many of the seeds of a successful program (see Figure 1-1).

The Vice-President for Human Resources at The Paul Revere, during this same period, was directed by the company

General Policy Letter No. 18   April 22, 1983
Subject: Quality and Productivity

General

It is a key Avco Corporation objective that it be identified both in perception and in fact as a high quality, high productivity company in all its business activities based on the following corporate credo:

- High quality and value of Avco's products and services for customers are the basic building blocks of its Corporate Strategy and critical components of its Mission.
- Maintenance of high quality, value and high productivity standards are at least equal in importance to corporate profitability.
- High quality and sustained productivity improvement are vital to achieving and sustaining Avco's competitive advantages.
- High quality and low costs are linked and fully compatible objectives.
- Competent employees are the most important company resource that can make the largest contribution to maintenance and improvement of high quality and productivity goals.
- Sustained corporate-wide activity, vigilance and concern with respect to high quality and productivity goals are a permanent part of Avco's corporate culture.

Definitions

- High quality means defect free, in conformance to requirements and doing it right the first time—nothing less is expected.
- Productivity means the rate of total true useful output produced per actual unit of total resources expended—simply put, the ratio of output to input.
- Value means the assessment by the customer of his satisfaction with the degree of excellence and the fair return he receives in products or services for his payments to and relationships with Avco Corp.

Figure 1-1. Letter from AVCO Chairman of the Board

President to find a way to improve productivity. The approach urged by the Vice-President's new assistant was Value Analysis, a formal, structured study of each major portion of the company to determine if each department is doing the right things, that is, only the things necessary to produce their defined product, service, or information. Some initial Value

Analysis projects were instituted on a pilot basis. At this point, any quality effort and the Value Analysis projects were seen as very separate, perhaps even competing, ideas.

The Chairman of the Board of AVCO and the head of The Paul Revere Operations Division (accounting for almost two-thirds of the Home Office employees) read and reread *Quality Is Free* by Phillip B. Crosby. It was the first book either executive had read that not only explained the concept of quality in a useable fashion, but offered some real examples rather than just theory.

The fact that the lessons and examples in *Quality Is Free* are almost exclusively from a manufacturing environment ultimately limited its use, but at least it defined some concepts, including a measure called the "Cost of Quality" and the framework of a possible approach. It was a substantial starting point.

Establishing a Committee

In response to the AVCO directive and fortified by new rules established by the Chairman of the AVCO Board of Directors, a Quality Improvement Team was formed. (One of the new rules was that any meeting with the Chairman would begin with a description of company quality efforts and progress.)

The Operations Vice-President was chosen to be Chairman of the committee, due to his interest in quality and his attempt the previous year to establish a quality program in his division. As a result of a tactical difference, that attempt had never gotten off the ground. Unlike the department head described previously, the Operations Vice President had asked permission of the president. The president had been willing to blink at the previous program, which covered a relatively small part of the entire work force, but he felt he could not sanction such a limited effort officially.

The composition of the Quality Improvement Team, later renamed the Quality Steering Committee (QSC), would have much to do with the direction and final definition of the quality program. It had to be powerful enough to make decisions or, at least, to make recommendations directly to the company president. It also had to be diverse enough to produce a final product that would blend all the best thought available in the company.

The newly appointed Chairman picked a committee composed of either the number one or number two executive in every division or major department. Fortunately, this included the Vice-President for Human Resources—the advocate of Value Analysis. The eight members occupied roughly equally spaced positions along an imaginary continuum drawn from "humanist" to "hard numbers."

Setting the Parameters

At first glance—and at the time—it appeared that the Quality Steering Committee wasted its first several meetings. Nothing noticeable was accomplished with the exception of the selection of a new company slogan, "Our Policy is Quality." The phrase coined to describe the ongoing activity was "messing around with quality."

In retrospect, these meetings were crucial. The points covered were: what does the word "quality" mean? What does it really mean? What does it mean to us? Having a common vocabulary, provided in this case by *Quality Is Free*, a copy of which was given to each QSC member, helped a great deal at the start. The discussions helped even more. One result of the meetings spent "messing around" was the birth of a distinctive vocabulary more broadly applicable to the company and its needs and culture. Several months later, when the employees were first involved, it was recommended to them that they too spend a few meetings discussing the concept of quality and its ramifications for their work units, using this vocabulary as a base. It was an investment that has paid monthly dividends since then.

The definition of the dual nature of quality is a product of these sessions. An expanded definition of customer—presented in Chapter 2—also resulted. The usefulness of both has been substantiated.

Subsequent discussions in the Quality Steering Committee meetings were heated at times. Perfect consensus may not have been reached on every point, but the surprisingly wide range of concerns that were argued as being a province of quality drove home to the committee members that (1) this was an enormous project; (2) done well, it had the potential to have an impact on all phases of the company, present and future; and (3) it would not be easy.

Armed with a mutual understanding of the ultimate goal, the next step was to examine practical considerations. *Quality is Free* again provided a jumping off point. As the final Quality Has Value process evolved, the fourteen steps outlined by Crosby to establish a quality improvement program were modified. Some became more important; others faded entirely. One step that was pivotal throughout the entire effort was Crosby's fourth step—"the Cost of Quality evaluation," which he defines as being composed of three elements: prevention costs, appraisal (or detection) costs, and failure costs. Some examples included in *Quality is Free* are:

Prevention costs: design reviews, supplier quality seminars, specification review, acceptance planning, quality audits, and preventive maintenance.

Appraisal costs: prototype inspection and test, supplier surveillance, process control acceptance, and status measurement and reporting.

Failure costs: consumer affairs, redesign, rework, scrap, warranty, and product liability.

When the Chairman of the Board of AVCO first read *Quality is Free*, he directed all units to conduct a Cost of Quality survey. It could be an estimate, a best guess, but he wanted to get a rough idea of the size of the problem/opportunity. An annual corporate figure of $288,000,000, which had been determined as the cost of ignoring quality, no doubt fueled his personal motivation. Breaking that number down into comparable sales and personal bonuses lost gave impetus to unit heads.

As The Paul Revere, the figure was determined to be $9,659,000 annually. The calculation and tracking of that figure are described in detail in Chapter 7.

These discussions were conducted in the vocabulary of a Quality Improvement Program. The Vice-President for Human Resources took an active part in them, but he also continued to investigate Value Analysis possibilities. Several consultants warned ominously against conducting any Value Analysis program in conjunction with a quality program. One even left his card, saying that if quality was launched before Value Analysis was completed, he would be available to come in and try to pick up the pieces.

Several conversations ensued between the Chairman of the Quality Steering Committee and the assistant to the Vice-President for Human Resources. These meetings were held to try to decide if, or how, the two ideas could fit together. The work force was, after all, made up of adults, and both ideas were aimed roughly in the same direction. Value Analysis, they decided, essentially aimed at "doing the right things"; quality, on the other hand, focused on "doing things right." Why should there be any difficulty merging the two?

It was more common sense than thorough research that was driving the thinking. Neither Value Analysis nor a quality program seemed to be particularly worthwhile by itself. The value of doing the right thing would be badly diminished if it was not done right; the quality of doing something right would go for naught if it was not the right thing to do. Since they seemed to be complementary notions, the decision was to do both simultaneously, despite the experts' warnings. The combination was given a derivative name that embodied this intention: Quality Has Value.

There was a recognition that practical considerations prohibited everything being done truly simultaneously. If Value Analysis did not get to Department A until several months after the quality program began, it was possible that time would have been spent improving a function only to have it discarded or dramatically altered later. It was decided that the merits of blending the two outweighed the difficulties.

Outlining the Plan

Simply telling employees to "think quality" does not suffice by itself any more than, in a social/political setting, it is sufficient to tell people to "think about the environment" or to "think about nuclear weapons." A format for converting thought into action must be provided. As Kivenko states, "High quality, after all, is not achieved by a few random management decisions but by a complex, all-encompassing, interactive management system that has the uncompromising long term support and involvement of top management."

In order to have an effect, the format cannot passively wait for the employees to use it, as is the case with too many suggestion systems. If it is to win widespread acceptance, it must be proactive and demonstrate to the employees that their ideas will count.

When QHV was launched on Friday the 13th, January 1984, it was the product of almost a year of planning. Figure 1-2 shows how the various parts of the program are related. Value Analysis workshops and Quality Teams act as the pivots. Quality Teams are composed of approximately ten people—a size congruent with quality circles. In practice, these Quality Teams function quite differently from their quality circles counterparts; a study of quality circles versus Quality Teams is presented in Chapter 4. Quality Teams, in turn, owe much of their success to adequate training of team leaders and to a program of recognition, gratitude, and celebration.

The theory behind each of these components is presented, along with examples, practical details, and descriptions of each component in action. The intent is to present not only *how* the plan works, but also *why*. In the final analysis, *why* may be the more significant since the theory can be adopted and the practice adapted without weakening the process.

The remarkable success of the Quality Has Value process in its first two years at The Paul Revere is detailed in Chapters 6 and 7. These chapters are a rich source of ideas for adaptation and implementation.

Chapter 8 provides a look at the new role of management. Traditionally, wisdom comes from the upper echelons of any corporate structure; procedures are devised and then defined for those lower on the ladder. The system applies at all points on the corporate spectrum. An employee, regardless of rank, listens "up" to learn and proclaims "down." It is a rigid, but conceptually simple, system, with the saving grace that it *appears* to work. It does not.

Dr. Deming believes that poor quality is "85 percent a management problem and 15 percent a worker problem." Val Olson, author of *White Collar Waste*, states that, "In the white

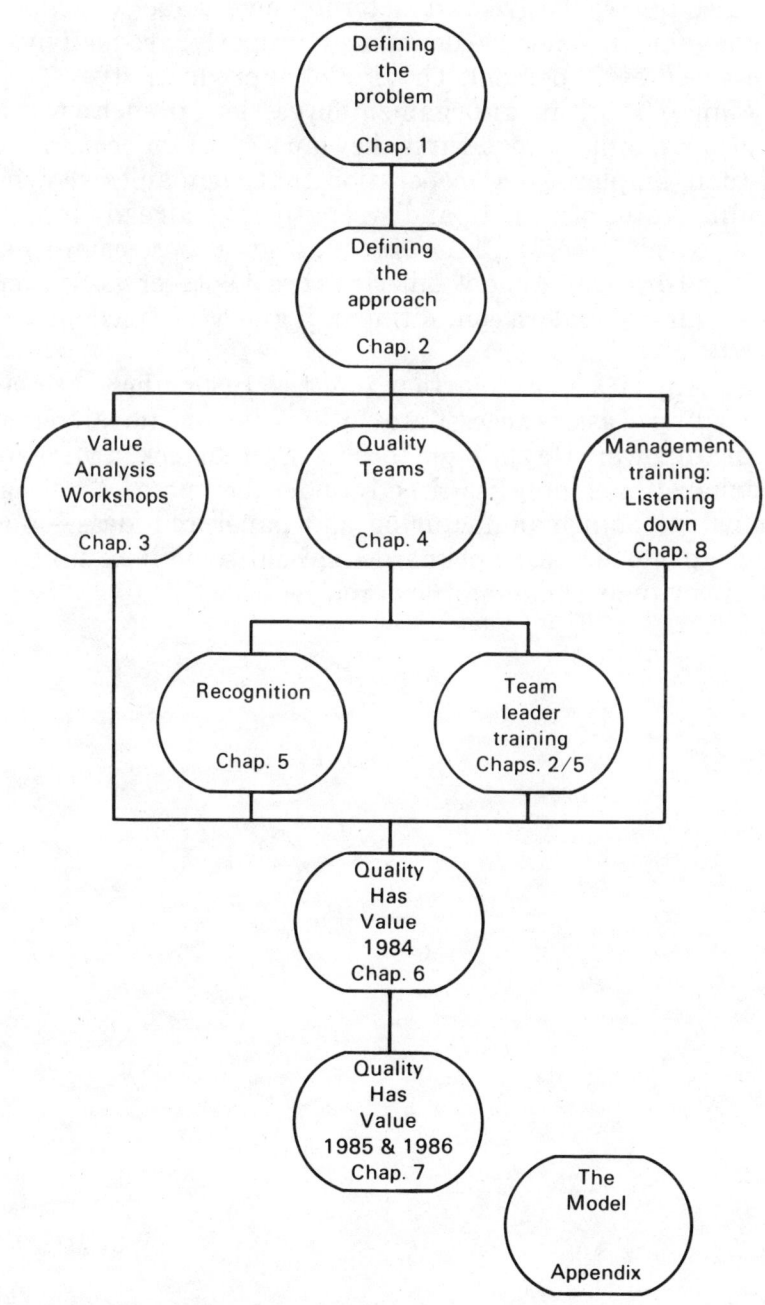

Figure 1-2. Relationship of the Chapters

collar industry the greatest factor for low productivity is poor management. When we do manage properly, productivity is increased by 50 percent. That's a lot of productivity."

Managers within an organization can lead in such a way as to insure quality output. First, they must enlist the cooperation of their employees, a cooperation that companies showing leading rates of growth and strength have already tapped. John Naisbitt, in *The Year Ahead*, said of these companies, "All had discovered one of America's best kept secrets: workers are aching to make a commitment, if given the freedom to do so."

As America moves further into the 1980s, the continued spreading of assets necessitates looking for additional sources of brainpower. Happily for those willing to look, a virtually inexhaustible supply lies directly under their noses. American industry—both manufacturing and paper-and-ideas—must now tap into the wealth of knowledge held, sometimes unknowingly, by their rank-and-file employees.

2

Quality Is Everybody's Business

Achieving quality requires the involvement of everyone responsible for any segment of making and presenting a product—be it a wrench or an annuity. Each person must be committed to achieving Quality in Fact and maintaining Quality in Perception. One surly person on your end of the phone can negate the work of hundreds of people and the expenditure of thousands of dollars just as surely as one weak bolt can ruin a multi-million-dollar engine. Conversely, George Odiorne notes, "If the people doing the job are involved and desire to improve the way things are done, they may prove to be a superior source of improvement."

In fact, a company's employees must feel that theirs is a quality operation, or many, including some of the best, will move on. Good employees have become increasingly mobile and quite conscious of their market value. They will need to be convinced that they are part of an organization that looks to them for help in becoming and/or remaining a quality company. And they will expect to receive quality service themselves from other units within the company.

The Quality Steering Committee agreed on this point from the beginning: any quality program would include everyone. It was a decision reached almost by default since it seemed so obvious. Based on a combination of rudimentary research on quality circles and their volunteers-only approach and on a statement in *Quality Is Free*, where Crosby admonished practitioners to keep everyone informed, the committee concurred that it just seemed reasonable to take an all-hands approach. There was no fanfare. The conclusion was not even included in the minutes.

In rejecting the volunteer system, the QSC did not, it appears now, realize how radical a decision they were making. Even the most progressive companies exclude their management level from measured, obvious participation. The message sent to nonmanagement by that approach is a discouraging one. Could it really be that nonmanagement is responsible for all the problems and management is already doing everything right? It seems unlikely.

Another point of equal importance seemed equally obvious. The company would be divided into teams, and the teams would be given a good deal of autonomy in implementing any ideas that they felt fell within their area of responsibility. Matching authority to responsibility just made sense. Was this revolutionary? Was it at odds with quality circle conventions? Perhaps, but it was also logical. The subcommittee that first proposed this approach was guided, at least in part, by the philosophy of the father of one of the members. The father, Mr. C. E. Langston, a high school principal in Atlanta, Georgia, had long taught that, "It is better to ask forgiveness than permission."

The "culture" of The Paul Revere prior to the initiation of the Quality Has Value process did not particularly foster innovation. A college senior, Judy Bleemer, described it this way in a research paper written in 1985:

> While the atmosphere within the company appears congenial and relaxed, things were not always this way. From its beginning in 1895 until a 1969 merger with AVCO, Paul Revere was a family run paternalistic company. Its officers were all Harrington men, a prominent Worcester family who preferred to keep the business within the family. While being paternalistic paid lower salaries to employees, it also provided more job security for those who were willing to trade off one benefit for

the other. The prevailing atmosphere was strict, stoic and what one would consider stereotypically militaristic. People were told when they could take breaks, use the rest rooms and smoke. However the last option was for men only. Women were not allowed to smoke nor were they allowed to travel for the company.

The decision to allow employees to become involved in the decision process was a break with the past. The Quality Steering Committee set the stage for what has become a permanent change in corporate culture. By including everyone in the organization and by letting all levels of the company make decisions affecting changes, the quality of The Paul Revere—in fact and in perception—was radically changed. Perceptions inside and outside the corporate headquarters underwent revision for the better. After the first twenty-four months, the cultural change wrought by the continuing process is evident. Chapters 6 and 7 detail these changes and include "proof" stories, true and apocryphal, which have been added to the unofficial collection of company legends, and "experience" stories from other organizations that have adapted practices from the Quality Has Value process.

Identifying the Customer

American workers have been told often in the last decade that they are slugs, therefore self-motivation has become difficult. The problem intensifies for those in a paper-and-ideas (service) industry; workers in a manufacturing plant can, at least, picture the physical thing for which they are responsible. For industries in which the products are ideas, rather than things that one can touch and either fondle lovingly or kick satisfyingly, it is tougher to relate responsibility to the final product. Understanding mechanical or physical quality is easier. If it looks good or tastes good or does not require much maintenance in order to do its intended "thing," it is quality. Relating ideas to quality is harder.

The key to the motivation of every employee, and the first step in involving everyone in attaining quality, is to give every employee well-defined customers. By expanding the definition of customer, the concept of quality and the contribution possible from each person become much clearer. The customer is not just the ultimate person or firm who actually buys and uses the firm's product or service; the customer is anyone to whom an individual provides any information, product, or service. And the customer *is* always right.

A particular worker's primary customer may very well be the person at the next desk or work station. The ultimate customers inhabit the outside world with money in their pockets; but the customers that the employee can do something about, those the employee can get immediate feedback from, may share the same roof.

With this outlook, the concepts of Quality in Fact and Quality in Perception become useful tools. Each unit or person can literally ask their customers how they are doing. This questioning can evolve into a concern about quality, about doing everything as expertly as possible.

One person's supplier may be another person's customer. Juran proposes that each person within an organization is a user, a processor, and a supplier. Each is a user, or customer, by virtue of being the recipient of a product, a service, or information in some incomplete stage of development. The role of processor may be taken on by causing some physical change, by the adjustment of some data, or by the addition of a valued opinion. Having completed the processing (an act that may take seconds or weeks), the hat of supplier is donned, and the product, service, or information is passed along to a new user, or customer. For success, the varying standards of all customers must be met.

As internal customers and providers begin to communicate, anomalies in internal Quality in Fact and Quality in Perception will begin to be discovered. One person may be working very hard to achieve a level of precision that is never again necessary or even considered. A clerk who spent an hour a week putting a stack of data cards in alphabetical order at The Paul Revere, for instance, noticed one day that the employee to whom she passed them on, her customer, was simply throwing the cards out without having looked at them. She had been alphabetizing the cards for over two years because of the instructions of her predecessor. The need for reviewing the cards, once real, had long since disappeared.

Any customer can be educated to take advantage of Quality in Fact that they have been ignoring, and thus negating; or the provider can scale back to less time-consuming (and thus less expensive) procedures.

A particular person or unit, by meeting what they understand to be their specifications, produces Quality in Fact, yet what they are doing can also fall short of the needs of their immediate customer. They think they are doing a first-rate job, but they are perceived as providing low quality. Resolving this type of disconnect requires tact and an understanding of the critical role of Quality in Perception. The placing of blame is not necessary—just a change in specifications to match the customer's expectations.

Weak spots in the linked chain of Quality in Fact can be discovered and corrected. By having everyone aiming to improve the overall quality—in fact and perception—of the company's product, within this user-processor-supplier framework, a company establishes an atmosphere in which the Quality in Fact chain can be strengthened with a minimum of hassle or excitement. Attention to people, inside and outside a company, commands the highest priority. If each person in the linked chain of quality treats the next person as a valued customer, the inevitable result is quality, in both senses of the word.

Publicizing the Effort

The first step in both informing and winning over the work force at all levels of The Paul Revere was an early letter from the company president, a copy of which was given to every employee. Although it did not contain many of the details of what was to become the Quality Has Value process, it made the potential impact clear. Dated August 17, 1983, it began, "I am pleased to announce the development of a long term and comprehensive Quality Improvement Program at Paul Revere." After saying that the program would involve all employees in the company, the letter went on:

It will have the very highest management priority because of its importance to the future success of our Companies. At a time when our marketplace is becoming increasingly competitive, a clear image of quality and an improvement in productivity through quality performance is vital to our position in the marketplace and to the service we provide our policyholders. This is not a "quick fix" program, but one that will be permanent, with goals established as we move through time. Quality performance and quality measures will become an integral part of each employee's job, including individual job standards and performance appraisals.

Quality, in terms of Paul Revere's products and services, can be described as "doing the right thing, doing it the right way, doing it right the first time, and doing it on time." To achieve this important Company objective, each of you will be asked to present your own ideas and thoughts on how best to improve the quality performance of our Companies. We feel that since it is you who are involved daily in and understand the wide variety of functions done in the Companies, that you can give us the best advice. I have appointed a Quality Improvement Team whose responsibility it is to establish a plan to achieve our quality objectives. A most important responsibility of this team is to obtain input and suggestions from all employees. This plan will be put together during the next several months, and we will begin to implement it in fiscal 1984.

You will be hearing much more about our plans during the next few weeks and months and will gain a fuller appreciation of how our new corporate theme, "Our Policy Is Quality" affects you personally.

The next step was a series of meetings attended by the members of the managerial ranks, instructed by members of the Quality Steering Committee. These were followed by department meetings held by department heads. The objectives of improving Quality in Fact and in Perception and the reduction of the Cost of Quality were stressed often. Also emphasized was the program's status as having "highest management priority" because of its importance to the economic health of the company. The program was described as both top-down and bottom-up, that is, top-down commitment and bottom-up implementation. It was also stated that the quality program was "developmental and emerging" and that it would take time.

Getting Outside Help

The conduct of the Value Analysis workshops, for instance, would be an experiment to the degree that the contracted firm, Nolan and Company, had never done them in conjunction with a quality program before. The President of the company, Robert E. Nolan, found the idea intriguing (some firms offering Value Analysis programs had expressed serious reservations at the least; others had offered to take over the whole program and do it "right" at most) and agreed not only to take part in the Quality Has Value program but also to send one of his lieutenants to the weekly QSC meetings so as to ensure as complete a fit as possible. The Value Analysis component of QHV is described in Chapter 3.

Another major point to be "developed" was the training for the team leaders. There was never any question that training was necessary. Team leaders would be required to conduct half-hour meetings weekly as the key activity that would feed the entire process. The meetings would have to be marvelously efficient. To commit, companywide, more than one half-hour a week was simply too expensive. Yet, many of the designated leaders-to-be had precious little experience at conducting a meeting and were especially shy of the skills required to lead a group through problem solving. This was particularly true of the lower-level supervisors who had one-on-one skills but not one-on-many.

Development of a training program looked to be a monumental task, but then some of the luck that blessed the birth of QHV (and often gave it the appearance of an accidental birth) showed itself again. The assistant to the Vice-President for Human Resources was charged with the responsibility of developing the training program. While investigating the possibility of putting together a program himself, he began a search of commercially offered packages. A friend told him that there was a California-based management development and training firm—Zenger-Miller, Inc.—that had a new product that might be worth a look. The program was titled "groupAction," and it was probably the easiest sale of their sales representative's career. It fit the criteria exactly. The use of groupAction is described with the discussion of Quality Teams in Chapter 4.

Zenger-Miller made a second easy sale when their representative came back several months later with "Toward Excellence," featuring Tom Peters. This course became a valuable tool in helping keep top executives focused on the objectives of the QHV process.

Refining the Details

By this point, there had been a subtle but important change in terminology. Quality Has Value would no longer, it was decided, be called a program. It was—and is—a *process*. The difference? A program has a definite beginning and a predetermined end, while a process does not have any ending, but rather becomes a part of the company culture. It is designed to bring about a permanent change in the way "things are done around here." Put another way, a doubting Thomas can hunker down and wait out a program but not a process. As seen in Chapter 4, it was a pivotal decision.

On a more functional level, the Vice-President for Operations invited the Vice-President for Human Resources to be the Co-chairman of the Quality Steering Committee, emphasizing the importance of the Value Analysis segment of the QHV process.

The "what" questions were, by and large, answered. The theoretical framework was spelled out, the training had begun, and a kickoff date of "around the first of the year" was agreed upon. There were still a number of "how" questions both unasked and unanswered. Enter a newly hired military retiree with the functionally vague title of Manager—Organizational Development. He started asking, "It all sounds good, but how exactly are you going to go about it?" About the third time he asked, the answer was, "How would you do it?" A mechanic was born.

Tracking the progress of the teams was the largest question mark. A Quality Team Tracking Program (QTTP) had been envisioned a few months previously, but no programming beyond the designing of a basic screen had been done (see Figure 2-1).

The Quality Team Tracking Program is a conceptually simple file program, available at any of the 150 computer terminals that crouch blinking in virtually every corner of the building. A plentitude of terminals is, of course, a common characteristic of financial or informational services organizations. Companies whose employees do not have ready access to computers will have to establish a manual tracking system—laborious, perhaps, but possible.

The file is formed by merging the team leader files, which required some tricky software. Each team leader can examine the entire QTTP file but can change only her or his piece of it. A team file consists of a series of formatted screens, each designed to hold one idea (see Figure 2-2). Aside from the team leader name and idea description, the important element on the screen turned out to be the team status.

Each idea is placed on a separate screen. When an idea is first entered in the file, the team status is normally set to "1," indicating that the team is working on it. If there is to be a delay or if a delay develops during the efforts to implement the idea, the code is changed to a "2." A "3" indicates that the idea, upon second thought, will not be pursued. The idea screen remains in the system in case, upon third thought, it is worth pursuing, or to serve as a possible inspiration for some other team leader taking time to browse through the system. In fact, "stealing" of ideas is encouraged. Once implemented, the status code is a "4," a designation decided on when the screen was first designed.

No one had decided how to use the data. To fill the gap, the new mechanic invented Quality Team Central (QTC).

The availability of people with specialized skills for Quality Team Central was another example of the good fortune that attended the beginning of the QHV process. For some time, four employees trained as productivity analysts had been responsible for conducting work analysis studies and work simplification projects, as well as conducting an ordinary suggestion system. The work measurement program, in fact,

28   *Commit to Quality*

```
Command ===>                 Edit SAS data set: QUALITY.MASTER          |Screen   1
                                                                        | Obs    13
|-----------------------------------------------------------------------|
                              OUR POLICY IS QUALITY
Team Leader: J. Ferguson         Cost Center:    77 Route # 105-02  Team No:  70
Team Name: The Grinches          Meeting Date: 11/12/85  No. of Attendees:  7
Item   Prty     Descriptions of Actions Considered or Taken
No.    No.
|-----------------------------------------------------------------------|
 67    ___    PROFS audit to be sure all ID's are in conformance with
              standards, all links are correct.
|-----------------------------------------------------------------------|
                                  ---Status---          Referred by
Effective Date  Next Action Date  Team   Other       Team No.      Est Annual Value
                                   2 *    **
|-----------------------------------------------------------------------|
      *  Team Status    active=1,   pending=2,   deleted=3,  implemented=4
      ** Other Status   higher=7,   lower=8,     other=9
************************************************************************
PF01 = Add    PF06 = Duplicate   PF07 = back 1   PF08 = Forward 1   PF12 = Exit
```

Figure 2-1. Quality Team Tracking Program Screen

```
Command ===>   Edit SAS data set: QUALITY.MASTER      | Screen   1
                                                      |----------
                                                      | New    14

              OUR POLICY IS QUALITY
Team Leader: ---          Cost Center: ---    Route # ---    Team No: ---
Team Name:   ---          Meeting Date: ---       No. of Attendees: ---
Item Prty     Descriptions of Actions Considered or Taken
No.  No.



                                         ---Status---          Referred by
                                          *    **
Effective Date  Next Action Date   Team  Other                 Team No.    Est Annual Value
       *   Team Status    active=1,  pending=2,  deleted=3, implemented=4
      ** Other Status     higher=7,  lower=8,    other=9
*****************************************************************************
PF01 = Add    PF06 = Duplicate    PF07 = back 1   PF08 = Forward 1   PF12 = Exit
*****************************************************************************
```

Figure 2-2. Completed Quality Team Tracking Program Screen

helped set the stage for the quality process by introducing the idea of measurement, analysis, and improvement of tasks. As the quality process began to take definitive shape late in 1983 and the need for some central point to oversee the mechanics of the process became evident, it also became apparent that much of what the productivity analysts were working on would soon disappear.

The suggestion system would have to be eliminated. If the two systems—the suggestion system and the Quality Teams—were allowed to coexist, some rather confusing scenarios could be the result. If, for instance, a Quality Team discussed a particular problem without reaching a conclusion and adjourned until the next meeting with the agreement that all the team members would think about the problem, what would prevent a team member from hustling to the nearest suggestion box with the problem and his or her individual solution? Trying to decide if a particular idea belonged to an individual or to a team would require the second coming of Solomon.

Since the intention was to encourage employees to think as a group, both as members of a small group and as members of the entire company, the suggestion system was scheduled to be dropped on the day that QHV officially began, January 13, 1984.

Teams were also to assume responsibility for improving and recording their own productivity. Once the suggestion system was cancelled, and the teams began working on their own, the productivity analysts would be looking for something new to do. The mechanic worked on convincing the Vice-President of Human Resources that the four analysts should become QTC with the responsibility of coordinating the tracking of the Quality Teams. Simultaneously, he spent many hours talking with the analysts about his idea for them and working out procedures for how to actually go about the task.

It was agreed that complete tracking of the changes taking place throughout the company had to be done. Thanks to the analysts' years of experience studying the workings of nearly every department in the company, they were the perfect ones to judge the twofold aspects of the problem. First, the aptness of an idea must be considered; next, and of greater importance, it must be decided whether the implementation of a particular idea had impact in any other area of the company.

Quality Team Central—composed of the mechanic, the four analysts (now quality analysts), and, later, a secretary—was officially formed in late December 1983. Their procedures were published in outline form a few days later.

The mechanical tool for tracking Quality Team ideas was already decided upon. By using the status code from the QTTP screens, QTC could see what the teams had been doing. At least once a week, QTC would get a listing of all the "4's" (implemented ideas) from the QTTP. The appropriate team leaders would be contacted, and appointments would be made. The purpose of the appointment was to certify the idea. Once certified, the team leader could change the status code to a newly defined "5."

Without the QTTP, Quality Team Central would have been swamped in paper. With the QTTP, the entire logging and certification process was reduced to two loose-leaf binders and periodic computer printouts. At the other end of the process, because there was no paper to be generated, team leaders felt much more inclined to proceed with "small" ideas—the ones that look unimpressive to someone three or four levels up the corporate wiring diagram but are keys to establishing a habit of quality. A by-product was the fun some of the employees had with their first introduction to computers.

The analysts loved their new job, particularly since they had instantly been transformed from the "bad guys" (whose presence in an area meant that work measurement—too often used as a club by managers in the past—was imminent) to "good guys," come to certify ideas and move a team toward recognition. Only "5's," ideas certified by Quality Team Central, counted for recognition purposes.

Recognition was a segment of the QHV process that was not defined until December. Chapter 5 gives a full description of the recognition scheme.

"Ready, Fire, Aim"

The pieces were all in place or, at least, enough of them were in place to get started. The important elements were:

1. Unquestionable and visible support from the top,
2. A high-level team with valid, mutually agreeable definitions and goals,
3. A general framework, and
4. A team of people to oversee the day-to-day functioning.

The whole procedure, particularly at first, smacked of "Ready, Fire, Aim." This may reflect the fact that late in 1983 *Quality is Free* had been overtaken by *In Search of Excellence* as the "philosophical" base for the process. The inexact, but determined, implementation was far closer to the Peters' model, with its emphasis on attitude and motivation, than to Phil Crosby's structured approach.

Some mistakes were made and quickly redressed. Some snags developed—the major one being that middle management seemed to have far greater difficulty becoming involved in the process than did top management or rank-and-file employees. The mental set necessary for middle managers in a quality process of this type and specific techniques that can be used are described in Chapter 8.

By early 1984, the QHV process was successful enough that the Quality Steering Committee was able to meet monthly, instead of weekly. The first-Thursday-of-the-month meetings were spent reviewing results presented by the former mechanic, now called the Director—Quality Team Central, and the Director of Value Analysis, examining proposed future activities, and establishing policy where appropriate.

QHV is still changing. One of the advantages of beginning a unique process is that no one ever knows for sure whether he or she may be doing something wrong, so little criticism is heard. The flip side, of course, is that you are also never entirely sure that you are right—until it works. It is a dynamic situation.

A detailed look at the component parts of Quality Has Value yields suggestions for anyone interested in achieving quality. As at The Paul Revere, it is a case of adopting theory and adapting practice.

3

Value Analysis

"Why bother doing it right if we're not sure we're doing the right thing? Why not Quality Teams and Value Analysis at the same time?" The question raised by the Quality Steering Committee echoes Peter F. Drucker's observation, "Efficiency is doing something very well. Effectiveness is doing the right thing exceedingly well.... What is the point of doing something very efficiently that should not be done at all?" Without a compelling argument to segregate the two efforts, The Paul Revere decided to merge the two into the Quality Has Value process. Value Analysis would take place; Quality Teams would be formed. The only question was the relative timing.

Quality Teams are primarily concerned with defining ways to do things right. Their analysis and study are normally based on the assumption that their departments are correctly structured; they work on improvements to that system. Given the amount of training and experience of most teams and the half-hour-a-week format, Quality Teams stay very busy concentrating on improving the quality of how things are done.

Value Analysis tackles the question of doing the right things. It can be argued that Quality Teams are less professional than many quality circles, because of their tendency not to get involved in proposing major projects that might bring structural

tural changes to a department. Whether that is true or not, it is true that the Value Analysis workshops go far beyond the scope of even the most energetic and knowledgeable quality circle. And it is the combination of the efforts of the Quality Teams and the Value Analysis workshops that ensures the future of quality in an organization.

Value Analysis is one of the permutations of what is often called value management. Lynn Tylczak, writing in *Piedmont Airlines* magazine, defined value management as "A function-oriented management technique that has been successfully used to cut overhead, production and administrative costs." In her article "The Concept of Value Management—Creativity Creating Productivity," she quoted Edward Lowe, Value Manager at Westinghouse, as saying, "Application of the VM techniques to logistics elements and systems could result in an estimated 25 to 40 percent improvement in costs with additional increases in quality, reliability and productivity." Tylczak goes on to state that "the concept of VM is simple, and even its most basic applications can create substantial cost savings or product improvements. When VM experts...take on a major corporate project, the results can be stupefying."

Using a Consultant

Outside help was needed to begin Value Analysis at The Paul Revere. Unlike the Quality Teams, which the Quality Steering Committee was satisfied they could define and establish, no clear plan for Value Analysis evolved. The Robert E. Nolan and Company of Simsbury, Connecticut was chosen to define and institute the Value Analysis workshops because of their track record of working with paper-and-ideas industries as well as manufacturing industries, and because of their willingness to work with the Quality Steering Committee. A representative from Nolan began attending Quality Steering Committee meetings—not only adding a knowledgeable voice to the discussions but, more importantly, ensuring that the Value Analysis format would fit into the overall QHV process.

A Value Analysis workshop consists of a group of four to eight decision makers from a single organizational unit led by a facilitator. Through a series of defined procedures, they determine the best way for that unit to meet its essential purpose. This is accomplished through meetings of approximately three hours, conducted twice a week for six to eight weeks, followed by implementation of approved ideas during the succeeding months. The Nolan consultants served as facilitators for the workshops conducted during the first several months of 1985. They also taught and then assisted The Paul Revere employees, who were to become the primary workshop facilitators as the process continued. The goal was to have value workshops be an in-house function as quickly as practicable.

Even with the restrained, integrated thrust of the Nolan employees, the reality is that there is a different reaction on the part of the workshop participants to an outside consultant than there is to a fellow employee who was there before this process began and will be there long after the workshop is over. No matter how good, how creditable, the consultant is, the suggestion of "hired gun" is impossible to dispel completely as is the thought that "we can wait this guy out."

There is also an aura of danger surrounding Value Analysis consultants. Much Value Analysis methodology leads to a reduction of the work force. This inevitably sours employees against both the outside consultants and the company's top management. One of the reasons for choosing the Nolan company was that its consultants were noted for assisting management personnel to find ways to improve quality through functional changes rather than reducing complement.

To minimize these drawbacks, a Paul Revere employee always held overall responsibility for the Value Analysis program. The difference between hearing, "You should do this to fix your company," and hearing, "We should do this to improve our company," is enormous. Most employees' commitment to a program or process is an accurate reflection of their perception of the commitment of company executives. Companies who have hired an outside firm to establish a quality circle program with virtually no apparent involvement of top management are handicapped from the start. This would also have been the case if outside Value Analysis facilitators had simply been put in place and told to conduct workshops, while completely ignoring the QHV process and the vital relationship of company employees to the conduct of the program.

There are unquestionably advantages to having an outside consultant on the basis defined. The Nolan consultants brought familiarity with Value Analysis procedures, objectivity, and knowledge of the outside world. As outsiders, the consultants were invested with the reputation of "experts"; company-trained facilitators would have had to earn that reputation the hard way. In the words of Robert E. Nolan, "The facilitator must be confident, knowledgeable, sympathetic, tough-minded, fair, and objective." Finding company employees to train as facilitators remained the responsibility of The Paul Revere. As the months passed, only one of the original six employees who began training proved able to be an effective in-house consultant, that is, combining the expertise and objectivity of an external consultant with the commitment and knowledge of a company employee. Another employee later completed the course, and these two conducted the Value Analysis workshops after the departure of the Nolan consultants.

Organizing a Workshop

A complete list of the phases of a value workshop includes: planning, information, creative alternatives, evaluation, recommendation, and implementation. The scheduling of workshops and the selection of participants constitute the initial steps in the first phase of a value workshop.

The scheduling of workshops was flexible enough to bend to the anticipated workloads of the various departments. Since it was a given that every department would take its turn before Value Analysis was over, the question of which department would proceed first was of minor importance. Once the workshop began, however, it was understood that all participants would attend all meetings. Carving out six or more hours a week for six to eight weeks from already busy schedules was not easy; however, thanks to the involvement and commitment of the top management, it was done. One obvious signal of commitment by top management was that superiors did not insist that workshop participants "skip just this one" meeting to meet with the executive. It reinforced value workshop time as having top priority.

The definition of who should participate in a value workshop was "decision makers from a department." This could mean supervisors or vice-presidents. The objective was to avoid reaching a point in the discussions where something of importance could not be decided because "That's Mary's area" or "Fred's the one who controls that." Mary and Fred were expected to be there from the beginning.

The planning phase also included the initial meeting, with its explanation of the Value Analysis program and an explanation of the procedures to be followed in the coming weeks. The facilitator explained the goals of the workshop and gave participants a common vocabulary to use.

The definition of Value Analysis given was: an organized approach to identifying what is needed from a function, and then redesigning that function to reliably achieve its objectives at the right cost.

The purpose of Value Analysis was said to be: ensure that departments perform functions that are truly needed to achieve the essential purpose of the operation.

The mechanics of the workshop were described. It was noted that the immediate product of the workshop would be a list of recommendations, and the long-range product would be the implementation of those recommendations. An oft-repeated point was that the only signatures that would be affixed to the recommendations would be those of the workshop participants. The facilitator's name would appear once, early in the descriptive portion of the workshop report, but the recommendations would be the sole property of the participants.

The importance of this was twofold. One was to strengthen the participants' commitment both to the workshop and to the resulting recommendations. The other was to stress that the workshop was not something being done *to* the participants, but something that *they* would do. The facilitator was just what the title implies, someone whose job was to facilitate the process by guiding the discussions, giving them format and purpose. The participants would produce the results, not the so-called hired gun riding off into the sunset, check in hand, while the survivors busily ignored the consultant's report and got back to real work. Even a homegrown facilitator would not and could not be expected to see to the implementation of the recommendations.

Continuing the introduction, a definition of the word "value" was next. This time, however, the definition was drawn from the participants. Like so many words, including quality, value is a word for which most people feel the definition, rather than articulate it. It was not an easy word to agree upon; however, in a business setting, most discussion boiled down to defining "value" in terms of receiving a fair return on an investment and/or monetary worth.

Participants were cautioned that they would be called upon to assess the relative worth of the various functions they performed. While it is possible to determine relative worth clearly when comparing two like items, it becomes an increasingly difficult and subjective concept as the nature of the things being compared diverges.

Part of the defining process was an understanding that some functions of each department might be eliminated. This was a good time to remind participants of a promise made by the President of The Paul Revere at the outset of the QHV process: nobody would be separated from the payroll because of the quality process. If in the interests of quality, a position was to be eliminated, its occupant would be offered another at the same or higher level somewhere in the company. The president went so far as to warn division heads that they might have to accept a less than ideal candidate for a position in order to keep this promise—but the promise would be kept. (This was not a guarantee of lifetime employment; termination for incompetence was still an option.)

As it turned out, nearly all reductions in complement were natural. When a person left for whatever personal reason, it was decided by his or her Quality Team whether a replacement was necessary. The other factor that aided in keeping the promise was that business kept improving. Quality products sell well.

To ensure that the participants understood that the workshop was not intended as a witch hunt, even though it was looking for waste within the company, obstacles to optimum value were explained. These included:

Lack of information
Lack of new ideas
Honest wrong belief
Lack of time

The workshop was structured to overcome these obstacles. It included the people who have the information to share. New ideas would be encouraged (if not demanded), and any honest wrong beliefs should be discovered and corrected in the course of the discussions. The problem of time had, at least for the next several weeks, been solved by fiat.

As the months went by, the track record of previous workshops provided positive information for the one in progress. "Success breeds success" is an experience-based cliche.

Arriving at an Essential Purpose

Definitions agreed to, it was time to find out exactly what the department did, that is, what functions each member of the department performed on a recurring basis. The emphasis was on functions, as opposed to tasks, with the latter being defined as a subset of the former. For example, a function might be entering data, while the supporting tasks would be completing code sheets, gathering information, sorting information, and typing data. As participants listed the many functions for which they had responsibility, a bonus from the Value Analysis workshops became apparent. They gained a clearer understanding of what each of the others did. Statements such as, "I didn't know you did that," "Are you still doing that?" and "My people do that too," were not uncommon. Determining the various functions of a department was a natural prelude to agreeing on their essential purpose or reason for the existence of an activity, unit, department, etc.

Anyone can write a few paragraphs or a few pages explaining why a department or individual should continue on the company's payroll. The explanation usually includes enough sweeping statements to allow for changing emphasis of effort over time or for providing an "escape clause" in case of unanswerable questions. Here, however, essential purpose must be stated in two words. One verb followed by one noun—no fudge factor. It is a gimmick, perhaps, but it is one that forces people to cut through all the smoke and get down to bare reality. The individual underwriting department, for example, passed over "make book" for the more decorous "accept risks."

The essential purpose agreed to in the workshop drives every subsequent decision. Discussion tended to be detailed and sometimes heated; settling on an essential purpose was not always easy or quick. One point that needed to be very clear before proceeding was the identity of the primary customer of the department under study.

In those cases where agreement was difficult or slow in coming, the discussion itself was of great benefit and presented valuable insights into the current work relationships within the department. It is very frustrating to find out that someone with whom you have worked for several years has a very different perspective on what is important about what the two of you do. It is also of substantial benefit, both to the workshop and to the future of the department, to get everyone in step on something as basic as the essential purpose of the department. When effort is being expended to do something that cannot be shown as contributing to the accomplishment of the essential purpose, the obvious question becomes, "Why is that being done? Why don't we stop doing it?"

Diagramming and Rating Functions

Dividing functions into primary ones—those that contribute directly to the accomplishment of the essential purpose—and secondary ones—those that made the accomplishment of the essential purpose possible while not contributing directly to it—set the stage for what amounts to a functional wiring diagram. Figure 3-1 is from the cafeteria at The Paul Revere and is included because eating is not an activity limited to one segment of the business world. Note that moving from left to right, each succeeding layer of activity answers the question "How?" Going from right to left answers the question "Why?"

Food Services

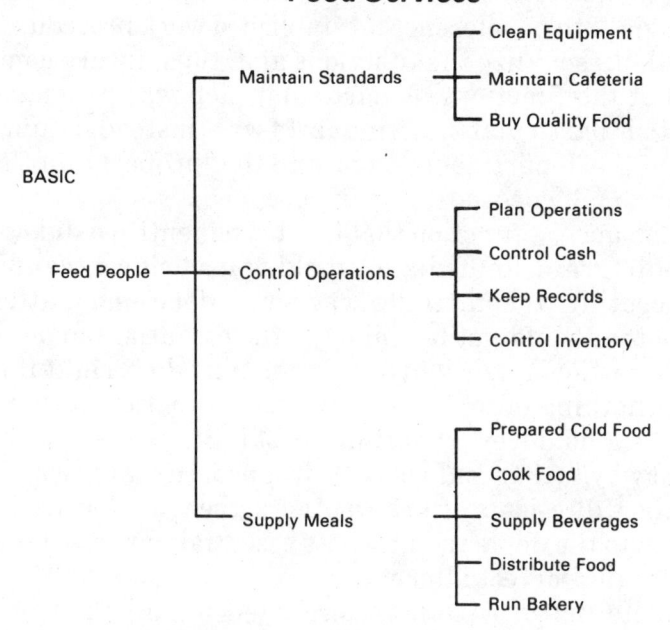

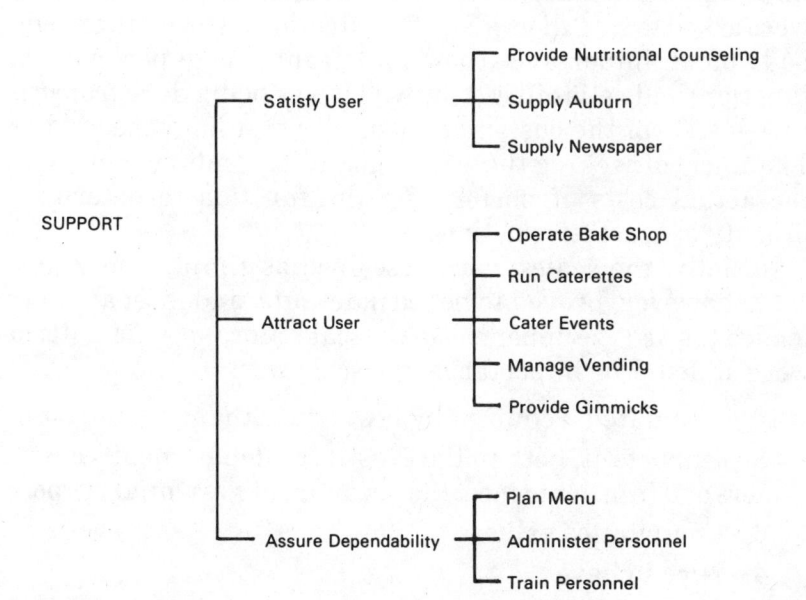

BASIC

- Feed People
  - Maintain Standards
    - Clean Equipment
    - Maintain Cafeteria
    - Buy Quality Food
  - Control Operations
    - Plan Operations
    - Control Cash
    - Keep Records
    - Control Inventory
  - Supply Meals
    - Prepared Cold Food
    - Cook Food
    - Supply Beverages
    - Distribute Food
    - Run Bakery

SUPPORT

- Satisfy User
  - Provide Nutritional Counseling
  - Supply Auburn
  - Supply Newspaper
- Attract User
  - Operate Bake Shop
  - Run Caterettes
  - Cater Events
  - Manage Vending
  - Provide Gimmicks
- Assure Dependability
  - Plan Menu
  - Administer Personnel
  - Train Personnel

Figure 3-1. Value Analysis "Wiring Diagram" for Cafeteria

Listing the functions in this way and basing the diagram solely on logic with no reference to established work procedures helped to depersonalize the functions and, thus, future comments about the functions. A particular step was no longer attached to a particular individual. It was, instead, simply one piece of the department puzzle and the "property" of the department, and workshop, as a whole.

More than once, a function that had been identified did not fit into the diagram, immediately making it a primary candidate for scrutiny. If something was being done—no matter how well—that could not be linked to the essential purpose, again the question arose: why continue? Why do it right if it isn't the right thing to do? In some cases, the function/activity proved to be a holdover from times past ("But we've always done it that way!") that could now be dropped. In some cases, it proved to be a duplicate effort. In others, the transferring of the function to the department whose essential purpose it did support was the correct alternative.

A complete list of functions accounted for all the work being performed in the department. Not all effort is of equal importance or value, however. Accordingly, the participants were asked to rate their identified functions. The rating would be twofold: importance (how important it is to perform the function) and reliability (how well it was being done from the perspective of the customer—whoever that happened to be). The object of seeking these ratings was to combine them with the actual costs of performing the function to determine priority of corrective actions.

Initially, the scales were described as simply one to ten. That, however, proved to be too indefinite, and most answers tended toward the upper end of the scale. More specific criteria were added. For importance, the scale was:

10—Mandated, required by law rather than just the boss

8—Important, both in the eyes of the department's customers and in order to meet the department's essential purpose

6—Contributes value

4—Nice to have

2—Limited value

0—Useless

The numbers 1, 3, 5, 7, and 9 were left undefined to allow for gradations. Importance ratings may not reflect customer interest. There may be some functions with high ratings about which the primary customer of the department neither knows nor cares nor feels the impact. The importance of the function to the corporation as a legal entity may instead by the driving impetus for the high rating.

For reliability, the scale was:

10—Perfect, a rare score

8—Well done, meaning the customers, when asked, cannot identify any real faults

6—Acceptable, when the customer will say there are occasional problems even if they are not particularly quantifiable; the problems tend to be changing and can often be traced to lapses rather than system weaknesses

4—Some problems, with some known deficiencies in the way functions are performed

2—Unreliable, meaning that the department cannot tell its customers with any predictable accuracy that it can produce the desired result

0—Awful

With the word and number scale, participants tended to be almost brutally honest in their evaluations, especially when assessing their customers' opinions of them. "We try," was a common statement, "but I know they think we fall short."

Cost could be determined objectively as a homework assignment. Costs included material costs, contract costs to pay others to perform their part, and wage costs for people-hours expended by the department. Again, being forced to tally all the costs for each function was itself a worthwhile drill.

One aid to using all this information was a graph, plotting each function according to its importance and reliability ratings. Functions that needed to be done but were not done notably well would, of course, be prime candidates for change-particularly if their cost was high. The opposite was also true. If, for instance, there was something that was not very important and did not cost much, then the fact that the customer was unhappy with the results would not carry as much weight as it might if it were a vital or expensive function. In fact, given those conditions, simply eliminating the function was an option to be explored.

Considering Options

Following these discussions, the most enjoyable phase of the value workshops, the creative phase, began. Participants were challenged with what if statements. "If you had unlimited funds and all the people you wanted, how would you improve the quality of your department?" While admitting that all ideas would later be subjected to real world analysis prior to making a list of recommendations, the premise for the next few meetings was that the members of the workshop "owned the railroad." Normal brainstorming rules prevailed, that is, everything was written down and no prejudgments were made. Suggestions that appeared bizarre were accepted as quickly as conservative ones. What might seem bizarre at first, after all, might contain the germ of a solid, useable idea or may trigger such a thought in someone else.

The approach of the creative phase was to take the defined functions one at a time and brainstorm a list of alternative approaches to accomplishing, in whole or in part, that specific function. When the group ran dry, it was on to the next one, although backing up was allowed. Two ideas appeared with some frequency: "Don't do it," and "Let someone else do it." In fact, if no one else offered those ideas, the facilitator would—particularly if the suggestion was needed to get things going. During the engineering and maintenance department workshop, one of the functions identified was washing the plastic trash cans by the night maintenance crew. "Don't do it" was followed by a practical suggestion: use plastic liners. Investigation showed that it was, indeed, less expensive not to do it. Plastic liners were cheaper than the cost of soap and water, even without counting the time saved.

The outpouring of ideas was staggering. This was one of the many areas in which the Value Analysis workshops and the Quality Teams augmented each other. Before the workshops began, the participants had already begun trying to examine their jobs in a different way. When the workshop was completed, the willingness and ability to reassess established procedures and the understanding of the concepts of quality had both been reinforced. This greatly accelerated Quality Team activity.

Just as the Quality Team Tracking Program was a boon to the Quality Team aspect of the Quality Has Value process, the use of a computer program greatly eased the paperwork of the value workshops. From listing and totaling costs to reproducing lists of brainstorming ideas to (eventually) tracking and totaling implementation of recommendations, the computer eliminated paperwork.

When the brainstorming was finished and hundreds of ideas had been transcribed into the computer program, everyone in the workshop began the evaluation phase. Everyone had a printout listing the importance and reliability ratings for each function and the many alternatives that the workshop had developed. Before the hard-nosed bargaining started, the facilitator would guide the group through a quick evaluation of the printout to cull those ideas that were not worth detailed study.

Ideas would be struck from the list if there was agreement that they fit one of the following categories: obviously impractical, illegal, counterproductive to the needs of the function, already in progress, concern of another operating area, or platitude. During this process, duplicate ideas were eliminated and like ideas were combined. Ideas that were deemed the proper concern of other departments were either put in a file, awaiting that department's value workshop, or taken directly to the department head for his or her consideration if the workshop was already completed.

The remaining ideas were then studied in detail, keeping in mind both the importance and reliability ratings of the function and its cost. As Tylczak described the general process for formulating recommendations:

> Employees at all levels of the company are taught to approach tasks and supplies with two questions in mind: what necessary function(s) does this item or task need to perform and what

alternative materials or methods exist that can fulfill the same necessary function(s)?

Often it is possible to identify less-expensive materials that can provide all necessary functions (for example, a lower-grade steel that meets all tolerance factors), find a material that can provide additional functions at the same cost (substituting a steel alloy that is of an equal price, can handle all necessary functions and has even greater wearability) or eliminate items or tasks that are no longer necessary due to system or technological changes.

The key is to focus on what needs to be accomplished—the vital function [or essential purpose]—instead of relying on the business-as-usual method of doing or buying.

Implementing Changes

Since the time to sign the list of recommendations was obviously fast approaching, the intensity of the discussion heightened as the ideas were fashioned into completed recommendations. It was not uncommon for a set of workshop participants to agree early in the program that they either would all sign the recommendations or nobody would. Minority reports would be of no use.

The facilitator normally would write the first draft of the workshop recommendations, but it would go to the participants for a set of corrections, modifications, and amplifications. Only the participants would sign.

The list of recommendations was then converted into an implementation plan, with specific people charged with the responsibility for carrying out each idea and with specific dates agreed upon. This list of recommendations and the implementation plan with all the signatures on it formed the basis for a formal presentation of the desired changes to the person next higher in the chain of command. The presentation was informational in nature, but it also served as the official request for a go-ahead before launching into the implementation. This was a departure from the Quality Team approach because of the scope of the recommendations. Normally approval was easily won, although budget and other considerations might affect the proposed schedule.

Returning to the unit with the list of recommendations was another area in which the Value Analysis workshops and the Quality Team activity paralleled one another. First, the idea of change, particularly change in the name of quality, was now commonplace. Second, the recommendations truly "belonged" to the decision makers of the department—in keeping with the philosophy of Quality Teams.

The two approaches also supplemented one another. While Value Analysis often made major changes as defined by the managers of the unit, it was often necessary for the Quality Teams—composed of the folks who actually did the work—to smooth the edges, so that the new fit would be a snug one.

The dual approach served to raise the quality consciousness of the employees. Seeing their bosses dutifully drop everything and march off to their value workshops twice a week for several weeks further impressed upon everyone that (1) the company is serious, and (2) upper-level employees share responsibility for quality (unlike the impression given in a company establishing quality circles).

Tracking the implementation of ideas and reminding departments of their commitments did prove necessary. This was not due to any malice or deviousness, but rather provides one more example of the truth of the saying, "When you are up to your hips in alligators, it is sometimes difficult to remember that you originally came there to drain the swamp." Decision makers would finish value workshops with recommendations on "how to drain the swamp," and the alligators would be waiting.

Examples of value workshop results in the first year at The Paul Revere demonstrate the versatility of the Value Analysis segment of the Quality Has Value process:

> Claims department: Increase the usage of arbitration versus suits, reducing legal fees by $80,000 a year.
>
> Actuarial department: Standardize the pricing and forecasting methodology used for all product lines to permit better product management decisions, producing over $400,000 in increased earnings.
>
> Pension services department: Contract annual pension plan

servicing to an outside service, thus saving $80,000 a year. This idea involved dropping nine positions; all nine employees were offered equivalent or higher positions within the company.

Individual underwriting department: Restructure the underwriting and issue departments from a production line to a team concept. Each team handled all aspects of the underwriting and issue functions for a specific group of Field offices. The new procedures allowed a customer to deal repeatedly with one team, thus improving customer service and saving $134,000 a year. Employees' morale was also raised, since they were able to see how their efforts related to the customer. This new focus on the customer in the Field was a result of a clearer understanding of the relationship between quality and customer satisfaction.

Group underwriting and group underwriting services departments: Merge. After group underwriting services completed their workshop, group underwriting discovered that they were covering many of the same topics. Group underwriting services participants were called back for a combined workshop. The two departments merged and adopted the same team concept used by the individual underwriting department. There were no complement reductions, but the combined workshop came up with another idea that resulted in a $500,000 savings. Procedures for setting rates were simplified, resulting in increased premium collections with less time expended.

Not all ideas represented big money—either in savings or increased income. Some cost money. But all of them addressed the basic question, "Are we doing the right things?"

Quality remained the primary focus, even though the potential money savings or gains were a very real consideration. As with the Quality Teams, it developed that in the majority of instances, an improvement in quality was also a plus on the bottom line. In five of the first thirty value workshops conducted at The Paul Revere, implementation of all recommendations cost $500,000. The other twenty-five value workshops, however, represented annual savings or additional capacity of income of $6 million. According to Tylczak, these savings are not out of line for a Value Analysis or Value Management program. She cites examples as large as $51 million (General Dynamics), $11.6 million (Army Corps of Engineers), and $18 million (Brunswick Corporation).

The combination of Value Analysis workshops and Quality Teams ensured that all obstacles to quality would be addressed—those that were institutionalized and those that were incidental. Quality is seldom quick; quality is rarely easy; however, quality can be achieved.

4

Quality Teams: An Improvement on Quality Circles

Ignorance can be bliss. While it is probably an oversimplification to say that The Paul Revere management thought they were creating quality circles but did not, it is true that the research was cursory. The original concept of Quality Teams was based in large part on the theory of Japanese quality circles, but quality circles that included everyone, which is a contradiction of the basic theory with unexpectedly positive results. The decision to include every employee in the Quality Has Value process drove many of the subsequent decisions and determined the unique procedures that evolved. Once that decision was made, similarities between the Quality Teams that were being fashioned and the Japanese import, quality circles, began to fade.

It was natural to look at quality circles as a prototype for action. A January 1985 article in *Harvard Business Review* estimated that 90 percent of the *Fortune* 500 companies had some form of quality circles. Yale's Center for Creative Leadership called them "Japan's productivity tour de force" in an article in 1981. Quality circles were riding the crest of publicity that had swept them across the Pacific and onto the shores of America.

The popularity of quality circles, at least in part, can be attributed to their being the best thing available at a time when something was needed to start the move toward getting American employees involved again in what they were doing. More importantly, quality circles moved management in America to admit that there was indeed wisdom residing on the lower rungs of the corporate ladder.

Carolyn J. Bigbee, a member of a quality circle at Hughes Aircraft Company, writing in *The Secretary*, pointed out that quality circles "verified that employees have a distinct desire to participate in avoiding, solving, and controlling problems that relate to their specific jobs," and that quality circles "acknowledge that each worker can contribute and that each possesses special knowledge, skills, and intellectual ability which may be applied to the work process."

However, like so many culturally based concepts, quality circles have not traveled all that well. In fact, a 1981 survey of Japanese-owned factories in the United States revealed only 20 of 238 had quality circle programs. Taken away from the paternalistic, job-for-life atmosphere of Japanese industry, quality circles just did not seem to be as effective as originally promised. Part of that is due to the numerous variations of quality circles. As Donald Dewar, President of the Quality Circle Institute, points out, "Quality Circles do not do things exactly the same way in every company. Many consultants teach a form of quality circles that is diametrically opposed to the theory as we teach it. Our 3,500 customers find that quality circles have vastly improved their operations."

Based on the number of failed quality circles, professional literature post-1983 began to shift from "Here's why you should" to "What's wrong with" when quality circles were the topic. Industry courses with titles such as "How to Pump Up Your Sagging Circles" began to draw substantial crowds. A paper written by Bob Richards of Consulting Associates International, Inc., begins, "As we watch the growth of Quality Circles in organizations throughout North America, we observe a growth in failures of the Quality Circle Process." By mid-1985, it was estimated by one analyst that 50 percent of the quality circles programs that had been started in white-collar environments had subsequently been cancelled.

An article titled "Quality circles after the fad," by Edward E. Lawler, III, and Susan A. Mohrman in *Harvard Business*

Review (January/February 1985), highlighted what the authors thought were major problems with quality circles. Low volunteer rate headed the list.

Fortuitously, the decision to make Quality Teams nonvoluntary created a hybrid that is not only thriving, but avoids many of the underlying difficulties associated with quality circles. The most obvious of these drawbacks is the reinforcement of an "us and them" mentality.

Virtually all employees of an organization do feel a degree of identification with their company. When the head of an organization leaves the building at night and later gets into conversation, the vocabulary is likely to include references to "my company." Anyone who has been with an organization more than two weeks uses the same terminology in talking with family and friends, if the relationship is a healthy one. The employee's feelings of proprietorship are far stronger than are those of the average stockholder. It is this feeling that "we are all in this together" that the Quality Teams concept reinforces and uses.

When there is a division between management and employees, the vocabulary of the employee is likely to be laced with comments about what "they" are doing, or what "they" expect from "us." Quality circles create another such schism. An average quality circle program will start out with four or five quality circles of about ten people each—even in a plant of several thousand employees. It creates a semi-elite structure that, under the label of worker participation, allows only a portion of the people within an organization to work on improving things. Now there is another "they," the good guys who joined the circles, the ones who volunteer up front to be a part of the solution to the company's problems. "Us" are the rest of the company, the slugs who apparently do not care about the future of the organization. "Us" are seen by both as "theys" part of the problem.

This "they" subgroup is not, however, a full-fledged member of the *other* "them," that is, the decision makers in the company. Quality circles are allowed to make recommendations, but the power continues to reside with management. Quality circles are given the responsibility to identify areas in need of improvement and to devise solutions to those problems. A presentation is then scheduled with a management committee to whom the problem and the proposed solution must be presented for approval. Commonly, the watchdog committee has two weeks to respond in writing to a quality circle with their decision as to whether or not to proceed with the recommended approach. No wonder the average quality circle in America only implemented six ideas last year. Their Japanese counterparts averaged between four and five.

Putting the definition of a problem and solution into one group's hands, while putting the decision to implement into another's, institutionalizes an employee versus management, us versus them approach. The members of quality circles no longer belong to either group. To management, they are still part of the work force; but to their fellow employees, they are a subset of management. The divisions are exacerbated.

Quality circles are further inhibited by the presence of a facilitator, since this is an individual not directly affected by the discussions taking place. The facilitator is trained to ensure that the format of the meeting stays on track while the circle leader is trying to work through the content of the discussion at hand. This monitoring of every meeting and presentation is hardly flattering to the participants.

Quality circles do represent a definite, progressive step toward getting employees involved in the organization and committed to better job performance, but they are only a start. Especially in America where the culture calls for faster action and a much greater degree of entrepreneurship (or, in this case, what has come to be called "intrapreneurship"), something more is needed.

The obvious step is to modify quality circles. By incorporating only forty or fifty employees in an employee-participation program, management severely limits the number of ideas and, thus, the potential benefits. In simplest terms, if a company can benefit from the monitored, bureaucracy-delayed recommendations of less than 15 percent of its employees, imagine the potential for gain from enlisting the contributions of 100 percent. As Admiral Frank Collins, U.S. Navy (retired), now the Vice-President, Quality Operations, Textron, Inc., puts it, "If quality circles have value, why not 100 percent? If quality circles have no value, why start at all?"

Involving Everyone in Quality

Quality Teams require a different mindset than that required to establish a quality circle program. For one thing, 100 percent involvement means that managers become team members, too—a tacit admission that they may not be doing everything possible already. By actively involving management, by encouraging them to be part of the company's effort to improve its quality, another wellspring of information and ideas is available. In a quality circle environment, managers are allowed to believe that they are not responsible for innovative improvements or may justifiably feel excluded; with Quality Teams, their obligation and ability to contribute is assumed.

Merely including managers on an organizational chart does not guarantee that they will be full partners in a quality process. A major service organization described its approach to achieving quality this way:

SENIOR MANAGEMENT. Its role is to establish corporate guidelines to insure that the employees and the Company are properly served by the... program.

COORDINATING GROUP made up of... staff. Its role is to assist in implementing and coordinating departmental... efforts.

STEERING GROUP made up of top department management. Its role is to develop department policies and procedures and provide resources and support.

COORDINATOR AND FACILITATORS made up of staff for the area conducting the program. Their role is to implement team action and train and coach the teams.

MIDDLE MANAGEMENT from the department. Their role is to review and support team recommendations.

TEAM LEADERS made up of supervisors from the unit. Their role is to conduct the... meetings and provide minutes and reports to the facilitator.

TEAM MEMBERS made up of employees from the same work area. Their role is to tackle and solve work problems.

Note that there are six layers of management—all to watch, to coordinate, to guide, to review, and to support—and only one layer of people actually contributing. The implications will be obvious to employees in the seventh layer: they are the only ones thought to be doing anything that needs improvement, but they are not considered capable of improving it without an awful lot of supervision.

The involvement of management in quality circles is taking an interesting turn in at least one company in Japan. The consumer loan company, AVCO Financial Services (AFS), has been initiating quality efforts involving 100 percent participation by its work force in its branches in the United States and Canada (Chapter 9). Its Japanese branch has had traditional quality circles for several years—traditional in that they included only clerical employees. Now, however, based on the enthusiasm and early success of the efforts in North America, management in AFS/Japan is becoming an active partner in their quality efforts.

The major way in which the teams differ from quality circles is forced by the "everybody is in" decision. There are no quality presentations to management. There would just be too many of them. By putting the decision, and authority, to implement at the Quality Team level—the lowest level possible—a good deal of control is sacrificed. There are quality circles that operate along similar lines. Dewar states, "We see no need to recommend that the boss approve an idea when it is within the purview of the supervisor to implement it. When that is the case, the idea should simply be implemented."

Quality Teams expand the latitude given in implementation. Even major ideas can be tried and then reported. The employees must be trusted to keep the best interests of the organization in mind. The gain in speed of implementation and in the number of ideas considered, discussed, and implemented makes the risk worth taking. If management truly wants all employees to be active participants in the quality process, it will have to relinquish formal control over implementation of ideas. The operative word is *trust*.

Given the chance, the overwhelming majority of workers want to have a say about their jobs. It is all part of the movement evident at virtually every level of American society. People want to be a part of the decision process, from free-agent ball players to voter tax initiatives. But they have not been challenged by American industry, and, as a result, their potential has gone untapped. They know this. According to *Technology Review*,

> Fewer than one of four jobholders (23 percent) say that they are currently working at their full potential. Nearly half of all jobholders (44 percent) say that they do not put much effort into their jobs over and above what is required to hold onto a job. The overwhelming majority (75 percent) say that they could be significantly more effective on their jobs than they are now.

This awareness can be translated into action.

As the employees are first led to understand the concepts of quality and customer and then convinced that their boss is serious about a long-term effort to involve them in the decision making, the outpouring of ideas will be staggering. John Naisbitt, in *Megatrends*, stated that in coming years, "People whose lives are affected by a decision must be a part of the process of arriving at that decision."

Quality Teams are built on the assumption that everybody in the organization is capable of contributing; everybody knows something about their job or the work of their unit that can be improved. It may be a small improvement but a series of those, a continual series of those, will have a tremendous impact on an organization, provided people are given the authority to make changes.

Training Team Leaders

Once it is agreed that a quality process will include everyone, several other formative decisions are made almost by default. One is that it will be impossible to have a trained facilitator at every meeting of every Quality Team. To do so would require a staff of facilitators of some magnitude. With most quality circles, all the members of the circle also receive training in problem solving and the conduct of meetings, with the quality circle leader receiving extra training. Again, when 100 percent of the employees are included, giving everyone in-depth training becomes excessively expensive—in terms of both money and time. The solution is to train the Quality Team leaders well and rely on them for both leadership and additional training at the team level. What is needed is a course that teaches the team leaders to conduct meetings in such a way as to elicit ideas and opinions from their people; Quality Team meetings are not a forum for the team leader to regale subordinates with the leader's great ideas. The course should also cover problem-solving skills, since the power to implement ideas is being pushed down the ladder.

The team leader, in effect, absorbs the duties of a facilitator. Since the leader is a member of the team, and will be affected by the decisions made, one of the potential weaknesses of quality circles is eliminated.

GroupAction, offered by Zenger-Miller, filled these needs. This course explains both how to conduct a meeting in a participative manner, (i.e., drawing ideas out of attendees), and how to solve problems by means of a complete problem-solving procedure. The useful format of the materials—both for instructor and student—sealed the choice.

The format of the instructor materials was of interest because Zenger-Miller would not be instructing The Paul Revere team leaders. They would, instead, teach a dozen or so promising Paul Revere employees designated to be future instructors. These newly certified instructors would then teach the team leaders. The advantages of this approach included: (1) it emphasized that the process was a Paul Revere one, (2) it enabled the instructor to include references to the quality process in the classes as appropriate, and (3) it was possible to make the course a regular offering on the company training schedule so that, in the future, new team leaders could receive the same training. Classes began in October 1983, with each team leader initially attending three full-day sessions in a month, followed by one session a month until the course was completed four months later.

To help convey the philosophy and the mood that it was hoped would characterize the Quality Has Value process, a video tape titled "The Pursuit of Efficiency" was added to the groupAction presentations. This short (twenty-six minutes) but marvelous British-made film portrays a tea lady who, while delivering tea and biscuits throughout a company, acts as a catalyst for innovative, bottom-up change.

A question asked on the first day of the forty-hour course helped to define both the need and the direction for the course. Used partially to get the conversation going, the question was, "How much time do you spend talking or working with two or more people?" When the class consisted of directors and above, the answers ranged from 45 percent to 90 percent. When the class was composed mostly of supervisors, the answers ranged from 5 percent to 40 percent. The former group would be sharpening skills and/or breaking old habits; the latter would be learning new skills.

One incident revealed much about attitudes before the beginning of the Quality Team process. During a groupAction class in which the students were primarily directors and second vice presidents, a vice president asked, "What if there is nothing to improve in our own area? Is it okay to suggest changes in other areas?" His comfortable assumption, of course, was that everything was fine in his operation.

Two days later in a class of supervisors, the question was, "When can we get started? My people are already making up lists of things they want to change." The supervisor who asked the question was in the direct line of command of that same second vice president.

The initial training program ran parallel to the Quality Steering Committee activities. The precise mechanisms for implementing change were decided upon after training began. Rather than the quality circle approach of presentations to management, followed by approval, followed by implementation, the Quality Team sequence became: (1) definition of area to be improved, (2) implementation of improvement, (3) notification of implementation, and (4) certification.

Certification of an idea consists of the team leader explaining the idea to a quality analyst and then proving/demonstrating its implementation. The basic question—besides whether the change has actually been made—is "Did this improve your Quality in Fact or in Perception?"

By talking through the problem and the solution, the quality analysts could determine whether all appropriate coordination had been taken care of and whether the idea truly represented an increase in quality. Once certified, an idea's status is changed to a "5" on the QTTP, and the idea is counted toward earning recognition.

Team leaders were told that the analysts would show them how to calculate savings the first time or two but that they were expected, as quickly as possible, to be able to do their own calculations. The analysts' role, it was explained, was to verify their figures, not to conduct the complete analysis. There simply was not time for the analysts to do all the research and calculations. As a result, team leaders and team members became far more conscious that time truly is money and were more likely to take opportunities to save steps.

As mentioned, small ideas are acceptable. The ease with which unspectacular ideas can be implemented is a real strength of the process. Since quality circle procedures are time-consuming, because the circle must thoroughly explain each idea to a management group prior to implementation, the very understandable tendency is to "go for the fences" every time up to bat. As any baseball fan can attest, many a player who swung for the bleachers on every at-bat had very few at-bats before returning to the minors. The players that last are the ones who have a good, consistent swing and who end their long careers with a mixture of broken-bat singles, bunt-singles, walks, and aboard-by-errors to go with their extra-base hits. Give a talented person lots of chances, praise them for their little successes, and the big hits will come. Guaranteed.

Since Quality Team members are not volunteers, recognition and thank you's beyond that recommended in quality circles become a greater factor. Recognition is such an important aspect of the Quality Has Value process that it is discussed separately in Chapter 5. Suffice it to say at this point that it far exceeds, without excluding, the quality circles belief that recognition and satisfaction come from controlling your own work environment and from interaction with management.

Establishing Teams

As the training of team leaders was progressing, the effort really began to sell and emphasize low-level decision making, one of the driving philosophies of the whole process. The Quality Team structure would be interlocking, it was explained, so that an idea could easily move up or down to the appropriate level, with the emphasis on doing it at the lowest possible level. Authority was promised, up front, to immediately implement any idea that could be defined as within the province of the Quality Team in question. While the authority may have been there all along, at least in theory, it was now expected that the authority would be exercised.

Another major aspect publicized early was the amount of time allocated to the process. Every Quality Team was to be allowed one thirty-minute period per week for a meeting on company time. Since there were 1,200 people in the Home Office, and about 10 percent would be on two teams, this represented at least a 650 person-hour investment per week—a sure sign of the depth of the commitment of the company to the process. It was an example of what had been designated top-down commitment and bottom-up implementation.

An element of fun was injected into the process by encouraging the teams to choose their names. The Quality Team Tracking Program sorted the ideas by team number, so the names could be as far out as the team members wished. The response was slow at first, but the names showed more and more creativity as time passed. Among team names were: Scullywags, The Dinner Belles, Marks of Excellence, Paula Revere and the Raiders, Bella's Bombers, Mighty Molars, Solid Gold Diggers, and the Lawful Awfuls.

Most had some twisted, but apparent, logic to them. One, however, required explanation. One of the two teams in the cafeteria was named "Faffanoose." It seems that the team leader was a notoriously poor speller and had, some years before, misspelled the name of the German Christmas cookie, pfeffernüsse. Spelled her way, it had since become an all-purpose word.

The Quality Has Value process was designed as a network of interlocking Quality Teams with an average of ten people to a team. The teams would be a shadow of the traditional organizational structure. Quality Teams would be composed as much as possible of people who worked together, and the supervisor (or manager or director) of the particular group in the normal scheme of things would double as the Quality Team leader. In some employee-participation programs, team members vote for their team leaders.

Having the unit head as the Quality Team leader made it easy to have a linking-pin arrangement throughout the Quality Team structure. Team leaders were also members of the Quality Team that was next up on the organizational ladder. Since the unit heads would tend to be both team leaders of one team and also members of their boss's team, it would be possible for ideas to rise or fall to the proper level for implementation. The result of these divisions was 127 Quality Teams.

Division heads were given general guidelines and were told to submit to the Quality Steering Committee the names of all those who would need to go through team leader training. Small work groups were combined and decisions were made about who should be the team leader, while large ones were split into more than one team with promising people given the opportunity to lead. In some cases, due to imminent transfer or terminal hesitancy, the "assistant boss" of a particular level group was designated as the team leader, and the boss was designated as a member of the team.

Using the natural work unit bosses as the Quality Team leaders meant they were in charge both during normal work and during quality meetings. This was one of the reasons that training in a participative meeting style was considered so important. Bosses at all levels were accustomed to holding meetings to pass information or issue directions—not to solicit thought.

This method of selection of team leaders was, in retrospect, the best way to start. Culture change is easier to accept if it appears to be evolutionary rather than revolutionary. The boss's active involvement at each level in the quality program further reinforced the company's commitment to the idea, utilized the boss's expertise, and gave the team members a familiar face in charge of things.

An opinion that supports this evolutionary approach is offered by Robert Townsend in his book *Further Up The Organization*:

Train your foremen to meet with their workers in idea sessions. Give foremen the authority to try ideas costing up to $150 each without further approval.

These sessions are efficient because poor ideas are shot down immediately by peers; good ideas get immediate support and stand a good chance if tried right away.

The wrong way: having workers tell an agent or delegate, who in turn garbles the idea in a meeting with other delegates.

An even worse way: suggestion boxes. Lots of people with good ideas can't put them down on paper and are afraid of looking stupid.

As the months rolled by, some changes began to take place. One team, which had been close to dormant for the first half of the year, suddenly had new ideas and was busy implementing them. Casual investigation revealed that the team leader, the supervisor of the group in question, had been out sick one day—the day a Quality Team meeting was scheduled. The team had held the meeting without her and, to their own delighted surprise, had gotten a great deal accomplished. When the team leader returned, she was asked cautiously, because she was both well liked and effective as a supervisor, if she would mind not coming to every team meeting. To her credit, she agreed to come only once a month and then to function as a member rather than the team leader. The team, the Class Acts (out of the actuarial department), had over fifty ideas implemented that year.

As the company neared the end of the first year, teams were invited to change team leaders for the new year. Special groupAction courses were scheduled to handle the 33 percent turnover. A sure sign that the hoped-for culture change was indeed taking hold came in looking over the new team leaders. Invariably, they were junior to the leader they would be replacing, sometimes several pay grades lower. The position of Quality Team leader was beginning to be seen as an opportunity not only to help the company, but to gain some personal visibility. New team leaders—the percentage of new leaders exceeded 50 percent by mid-1985—continuously revitalize the process.

Achieving Results

When the Quality Team process started in early 1984, a few heroes quickly emerged. In the financial services area, a recently hired level 3 clerk, while learning her job, realized that the company policy was to maintain a zero dollar balance in its many checking accounts around the country. The accounts were used for payment of rent on local office space and other local expenses. The zero-balance policy had no doubt been established years ago, before the days of interest-bearing NOW accounts, free checking for maintaining a defined minimum balance, and heavy penalties for overdrafts. Since the policy did not make much sense to the young lady, she took time to figure out what it was costing the company in penalties, charges, and interest lost. The figure came to just over $3,000 a year.

Her next stop was the Quality Team leader, who was easily convinced. They immediately went to the vice-president for financial services. He looked at the figures, quickly did some calculations of his own that raised the potential savings to $5,000 a year, and said, "You're right. Change the policy today."

The money was shifted into the accounts the next day, the signal was sent that "we" can really change things, and the Quality Team—the Deadliners—that counted the young clerk as one of its members went on to win Most Valuable Team honors at the end of 1984.

At virtually the same time, in another part of the building, the Quality Team leader in the key punch department oversaw a discussion among her team members that also helped get the process off to a running start. The key punch operators had, in the past, literally been told not to think. "Just type what's there—don't think about it," was the rule. As a result, they had been inputting errors and working with inefficiently designed formats for years; and as they typed in a given set of data, they would think, "That should be a '4,' not an 'L.' I'll see this one again in a few days."

And, of course, they did. The computer cards would be fed into the computer, an error message would be generated, it would sit in the programmer's in basket for a day or two, be corrected, and returned to the key punch operator with the correct "4." It was all very wasteful; but it was the way things were done. Now the operators were told that they were not only being allowed to think, it was expected. They quickly decided to address the problem of obvious errors on the coding sheets that they received.

The chance to put their new plan into action came quickly. An operator spotted an apparent error on a coding sheet. As was the case in most instances, she knew only that it was wrong. She had no way of knowing what the correct entry should be.

A telephone call to the programmer elicited this response, "Oh, well, go ahead and just type it the way it is. I'll correct it when it gets back to me."

"No," was the answer. "It'll only take a moment to come here and correct this. Otherwise we're both going to have to spend a lot more time on it a few days from now."

A silence was followed by an obviously amazed, "You're right, I'll be right there." The team, dubbed Goldfingers, was the first to have twenty-five ideas certified and was a leader throughout the year.

Not all teams were immediately active, of course. A disadvantage of having 100 percent involvement is that not every team member is deeply committed—or even marginally committed—at the outset. Most teams had a mixture of enthusiasts and cynics, of those willing to get involved right away and those who were sure this was just another "program of the month" that would soon go away.

This mixture has its advantages. For one thing, it keeps those who might get excessively Pollyanaish from straying too far from the real world. Having a built-in devil's advocate keeps any group a little more honest and realistic. Another advantage is that many initial cynics did come around and, frequently, just about the time that the early converts had almost exhausted their first pile of ideas. The cynics may claim that they still did not "buy all this stuff," but were, rather, just "taking advantage" of the system to improve their own work conditions. After watching one's fellow workers take care of all those petty annoyances, even the most cynical will give it a try. This is the first step toward conversion. To paraphrase (liberally), while you might not be able to make a horse drink after you lead it to water, you can hold his head near the water, explain how good the water tastes, remind it just how long it has been since the last drink, and let it watch the other horses drinking their fill.

The nice part is that when a person decides that maybe, just maybe, there is something there worth trying, they do not have to ask in, they are already there. They are attending Quality Team meetings. All they have to do is speak up. With quality circles, if a person is a late convert, they frequently must wait until there are enough volunteers to form a new circle or until there is a facilitator to help the circle get started and function.

If the goal is quality, and, more specifically, to reach a point where everyone in the organization is continually searching for ways to improve their or the company's Quality in fact or Quality in perception—making it difficult to contribute is counterproductive.

Quality Teams—Beyond Quality Circles

Perhaps the best description of the relationship between quality circles and Quality Teams is that Quality Teams are the next evolutionary step beyond quality circles. They are a blend of quality circles, suggestion systems, participative management, and Yankee ingenuity. And they may be closer to what Dr. Deming had in mind in the first place. An American Productivity Center report states that,

> The basic idea that Deming had is this: If management is to be responsible for improving something as complicated as modern assembly of machines and people (whether in the factory, the hospital, the office or anywhere), managers must have a way of learning (1) which parts of the problems are due to the workers and (2) which parts are due to the system.

Making everybody responsible for improving something via Quality Teams provides the way.

The flaws that Lawler and Mohrman identify in "Quality circles after the fad" are not inherent in all quality circles, but they create a framework for discussing why quality circles fall short of expectations in so many American companies. These "Destructive forces" that can doom a quality circle program (see Figure 4-1) also provide a basis to study the specific ways in which Quality Teams compensate for these weaknesses. The chart has been extended to include the Quality Team approach to each of the seventeen points (see Figure 4-2).

The first point, the low volunteer rate, is, of course, not a problem with Quality Teams. What must be done instead of motivating people to volunteer is to convince them that the fact that they have been "volunteered" works in their favor. From the very beginning, the long-range goal of a change in corporate culture must be stressed and repeated. One way to approach this is to create an awareness that Quality Teams are part of a process not a program.

As discussed in Chapter 2, "program" implies a plan of action that has a definite beginning and a definite end. A "process," on the other hand, has no particular end. It is, instead, a change in "the way we do things around here," a change that becomes a permanent part of the day-to-day work habits, a change in corporate culture. This explanation is the foundation of why everyone has been "volunteered," and it must be publicized.

Lawler and Mohrman also refer to a lack of adequate funding. Clearly, with everyone in the company involved, a commitment to adequate funding is one of the foundations of success. The installation of a quality process such as that described in this book is not cheap. The return on investment, once the process is rolling, will satisfy even the greediest stockholder, but it will take some faith up front—faith in the employees to both know how to improve things and to be willing to share that knowledge once the forum is provided.

It will cost in people to run the process; it will cost in time devoted first by the steering committee and then, on an ongoing basis, by the teams in their meetings; it will cost to do the training; and it will cost to run a recognition program. Correctly established, costs will be returned quickly. At The Paul Revere, the costs for recognition alone in the first year were $80,000, but the annualized savings were over $3.25 million.

Training is every bit as important to Quality Teams as it is to quality circles. By restricting the formal training to team leaders, trust in those team leaders is being exhibited. Knowing that new team leaders can, and will, be trained in the future broadens the base. Besides the cost, the correct thrust of the training is vital. There should be a recognition that the skills necessary for conducting meetings and solving problems are merely a starting point. The presumption that there is only one correct way to conduct meetings and institute change must be abandoned, and specific skills must be mastered on an as-needed basis. Tell the employees that you want a bearskin coat. Expose them to guns, bows and arrows, traps, poisons, and clubs. Let them decide which to use.

The Lawler-Mohrman article also identified weaknesses in the initial problem solving phase. Disagreement on problems becomes far less contentious when solution to any problem—large or small—is encouraged. By heavily advertising the process as something that will be a part of the company until the walls come tumbling down, the pressure to "do mine first" also decreases considerably. After a first series of ideas or areas to be improved are identified, the group can prioritize them and start down the list, confident that the last one on the list will, in time, be addressed.

Lack of knowledge of operations is less of a potential problem with Quality Teams, since, in the majority of cases, the decisions are implemented in the department in which the team works. The team, therefore, is the expert on what to change. On those decisions that cross departmental lines, the quality analysts can act as coordinators, or a designated team member can go to the duty expert and ask the right questions. As the first year progressed at The Paul Revere, the word "quality" became a velvet club. Previously, if a person walked into someone's office and said, "I've got an idea I'd like to talk about," they stood a fair chance of being scheduled sometime near the end of the decade. Now, however, if the opening line is, "I've got a quality idea, and my team would like some information," the response is almost always, "Let's talk about it. What do you need?" Obviously, top-down commitment is not just a plus, it is imperative.

Quality Teams: An Improvement on Quality Circles 69

Phase	Activity	Destructive forces
Start-up	Publicize Obtain funds and volunteers Train	Low volunteer rate Inadequate funding Inability to learn group-process and problem-solving skills
Initial problem solving Approval of initial suggestions	Identify and solve problems Present and have initial suggestions accepted	Disagreement on problems Lack of knowledge of operation Resistance by staff groups and middle management Poor presentations and suggestions because of limited knowledge
Implementation	Relevant groups act on suggestions	Prohibitive costs Resistance by groups that must implement
Expansion of problem solving	Form new groups Old groups continue	Member-nonmember conflict Raised aspirations Lack of problems Expense of parallel organization
Decline	Fewer groups meet	Savings not realized Rewards wanted Cynicism about program Burnout

Figure 4-1. "Destructive Forces" with Quality Circles

70   Commit to Quality

Phase	Activity	Destructive forces	Quality team
Start-up	Publicize Obtain funds and volunteers	Low volunteer rate Inadequate funding	Nonvolunteer Expected expense justified by expected return
	Train	Inability to learn group-process and problem-solving skills	Only team leaders trained; stress on attitude and concept
Initial problem solving	Identify and solve problems	Disagreement on problems Lack of knowledge of operations	Team prioritizes; all suggestions studied With everybody on a team, knowledge is available
Approval of initial suggestions	Present and have initial suggestions accepted	Resistance by staff groups and middle management Poor presentations and suggestions because of limited knowledge	Overcome by momentum from below and commitment from above No presentations; teams concentrate on problems they can solve

Figure 4-2. Quality Team Solutions

Implementation	Relevant groups act on suggestions	Prohibitive costs	Costs justified by benefits, if it is to be implemented Sharing credit for ideas makes for partners, not adversaries
Expansion of problem solving	Form new groups Old groups continue	Resistance by groups that must implement Member-nonmember conflict Raised aspirations Lack of problems	No nonmembers Aspirations met Recognition that improvement is always possible Justified by results
		Expense of parallel organization Savings not realized	Savings precede recognition Rewards given
Decline	Fewer groups meet	Rewards wanted Cynicism about program Burnout	Process becomes a part of routine Evolves into part of corporate culture

Figure 4-2. (continued)

Top-down commitment is also necessary to overcome the natural resistance of middle managers. This is a real problem but not an insurmountable one. Chapter 8 suggests one approach to overcoming this stumbling block to changes in corporate routine. There is less opportunity for middle managers to block initiative and change with the Quality Team approach than there is with quality circles. Presentations cease to be a problem, since there are none. Poor suggestions still arise, but they tend to be an insignificant percentage of the total number of ideas. Quality Teams are self-policing.

Costs of implementing ideas should not present any special or new problems. First of all, the overwhelming majority of the ideas will have no implementation costs or will generate immediate savings. There need be no separate budget for implementing quality ideas. Each idea with costs attached must compete for funds with the other priorities facing the same department. Those with large implementation costs must undergo the same scrutiny that any idea would, whatever the source. If the return on investment is good, and provable, then good business sense dictates its implementation.

Ideas that involve more than one team do not meet with the same degree of resistance that the us versus them quality circle approach breeds. Since everyone is on a team, and since any team may need help implementing an idea at some point, mutual cooperation is in everyone's best interest. By establishing the idea of sharing ideas (for which both teams can earn credit toward recognition), most resistance to implementation is eliminated. Being enlisted as a partner always engenders good will.

The six destructive forces listed under the expansion of problem solving phase in Figure 4-1 are also answered by the recommended Quality Team process. There is no member-nonmember conflict since, by definition, there are no nonmembers. The raised aspirations that the Lawler-Mohrman article refers to are those that come from being an equal member in a quality circle and then losing that status when working with members not in a circle. Since Quality Team members work together, and since the unit manager is usually a member of the same team, many of the raised aspirations can be met. As everyone becomes aware of the abilities of their fellow workers, mutual respect grows. A common vocabulary for problem solving develops, and since the process is aimed at a change in corporate culture, the treatment received in the role of the Quality Team member will become the norm.

As habits of quality are established, there is an accompanying recognition that there is always room for improvement. The results of the Quality Has Value process in its first two years indicate that teams can always find a problem to solve.

The cost of the parallel organization represented by the Quality Teams is the cost in time away from their normal duties. This time, however, is being used in an extremely productive manner—the savings from which more than offset the time used. The savings are realized because the process is structured to result in quick, if not instantaneous, results. As was seen in Chapter 3, most major changes that, by their nature, take longer to set in place come from the Value Analysis portion of the Quality Has Value process.

The listing of rewards wanted as a flaw of quality circles also points to an interesting bias. Why shouldn't there be rewards? Why shouldn't rewards be both psychological and tangible? Virtue need not necessarily be its own reward, and Chapter 5 suggests some alternatives.

Making a Commitment

The last two flaws, cynicism and burnout, have a lot to do with the way in which quality circle programs have been used in this country. Quality circles can produce positive results; but they start out handicapped by the very things that initially make them attractive. After pointing out the large-scale introduction of quality circles in the last several years, Lawler and Mohrman credited their popularity to four factors: (1) they are accessible (i.e., a "package" can now be purchased), for a fixed price a consultant will come in and establish quality circles for the company in question; (2) they "do not have to involve everyone, so small scale experiments can be run"; (3) the circles "have no decision-making power" so "managers don't have to give up any control or prerogatives" and, besides, "top management can easily eliminate them if they become troublesome"; and (4) they are the fad and are tried simply because they currently symbolize "modern participative management."

A decision to introduce a Quality Team concept must be based on diametrically opposed reasoning. No outside consultant can be relied on to establish Quality Teams for a company. One might help initiate the process, and aim it in the right direction, but without the time-consuming effort and commitment of the highest level of management in the unit to be improved, the effort will be for naught. Changes in corporate culture cannot be hired out.

The hiring of an outside firm to come in and run an employee-participation program is consistent with the paternalistic management style that gave birth to the whole quality circle movement. It is as if the parents of a disappointing child hired a new nanny to make the kid feel like a member of the family without the investment of anything except money on the part of the parents. Besides, if things do not work, the blameless parents can fire the incompetent nanny.

Limiting involvement to a few employees has the same kind of attraction for some companies. A few employees cannot be too big a bother—or too big a benefit. If management believes that the involvement of the employees will benefit the growth and strength of the company, then it is illogical to limit the possible gain by excluding 90 percent of the work force. If the intention is to look like a benevolent company, to make the employees feel good, but not be bothered too much by them, then fine. The "attraction" of not having to actually surrender any decision-making power reinforces this half-hearted approach. In this context, quality circles are *done to* employees by management; Quality Teams are *done by* employees and management together.

The four "attractions" of quality circles listed by Lawler and Mohrman are the roots of the burnout and cynicism that are its fatal flaws. There is something very basic in the makeup of the Quality Team process that ensures that it does not share these flaws. Everybody in the organization is an active participant in the process, and it is understood from the outset that all the mechanics are leading to a permanent change in the corporate culture. Some of the mechanics may need to be adjusted as time goes by, but if the changes in attitude have truly been taking place, growth and change will continue.

Quality circles have, without doubt, been of benefit to American industry. Their limited application (as shown by their emphasis on manufacturing industries to the exclusion of service industries) and their limited membership (volunteers, and not too many of them) ultimately inhibit their value.

A decision to institute a Quality Team process is, if you will, a decision to allow a revolution. Revolutions come from the bottom up. If there is to be a new American revolution, service industrial revolution, all the troops must be enlisted. It will be a benign revolution. The Bureau of National Affairs, Inc., states that its data show that "giving workers a voice in management of work promises to increase the individual's concern for the product and the process and to generate higher productivity and quality."

5

Virtue Is Not Necessarily Its Own Reward

While chronologically the recognition, gratitude, and celebration components of the Quality Has Value process were among the last pieces of the process to be defined, their importance cannot be overemphasized. The costs are high in time and money, but the return more than justifies the expense. Benefits come not only in provable revenue generated, anticipated costs reduced, and in measurable increases in quality. There are more abstract benefits. The employees' attitude about themselves and *their* company change as they see themselves as competent, appreciated members of an organization involved in something challenging, exciting, and fun—a company that is able to say thank you in ways that they understand. That attitude is a major step toward establishing a corporate culture in which quality is the norm.

There are, not surprisingly, many theories on how best to recognize or reward or merely take note of, an employee's contributions in a process or program such as the one discussed in this book. At one end of the scale, there is the method used by most quality circles, which emphasizes recognition, that is, public acclaim and honor. At the other, there is the incentive approach used in conjunction with most suggestion systems, that is, a percentage of the profits/savings that result from an idea.

There are flaws in both the quality circles "virtue is its own reward" approach and the suggestion system, score-keeping approach that act as built-in barriers to inculcating the company as a whole with a habit of quality. For one thing, both encourage concentration on ideas that have major impact. The quality circles emphasis on big ideas comes from the requirement that a management committee give permission to make the improvements they propose. The suggestion system, while there is often a minimum payment, is obviously geared to money-saving ideas, and the bigger the better.

The fact is, however, that no one approach will act to motivate every individual. This is attested to by the low number of volunteers for quality circles and the low percentage of employees who participate repeatedly in any suggestion system. When the goal is the involvement and motivation of an entire work force, there must be another way. What is presented in this chapter is a method for blending elements of recognition, gratitude, and celebration into a program for thanking employees while acting as a motivator for further commitment. The program is based on accepted management theory, *and* it works.

Understanding Maslow's Theory

Virtually every basic course in management taught in America includes an explanation of the Maslow "hierarchy of needs." The points are memorized for tests and then, all too often, forgotten. Yet, it explains why two people will react differently to the same stimuli and why the same person may react differently to the same stimuli at different times.

Depending upon their personal development and perceived status in life, people will attach particular values to items or actions offered by a company. This simple distillation of Maslow's theory explains why a program that offers a combination of recognition, gratitude, and celebration is so successful. For some people, public acknowledgment or recognition of their value to the company will be the primary motivator. For others, material awards are the primary source of inspiration and motivation. And for others, the celebration that attends both the recognition and gratitude will be what turns them on. For most, a combination will work best.

The idea that different people hear "thank you" in different ways should be no surprise. In fact, a look at the Maslow need hierarchy indicates that any other reaction to a recognition/gratitude program would be the real surprise.

The Maslow need hierarchy states that every human has the same basic needs and will strive to fill these needs in a generally sequential manner. The needs as set out by Maslow are:

1. Physiological
2. Safety and security
3. Belongingness, and love
4. Autonomy and self-esteem
5. Self-actualization.

The progression from one level to the next is not a nice, neat one. People do not put all their energies into meeting just one level of needs and, those needs satisfied, begin concentrating solely on the next higher level of needs.

It is, rather, closer to the acts that used to be featured on the "Ed Sullivan Show" in which the performer would attempt to get a whole series of dinner plates twirling atop long, slender rods. While the difficult and crucial point comes in getting any one plate spinning comfortably on its thin pillar, maintenance must be performed on the ones that are already spinning. At the same time the performer must be thinking about how to get the next one in the air. It would not have impressed Ed Sullivan, or anyone else, to get a fourth or fifth plate up if the first three had already crashed to the stage.

While any one person's primary focus will be on one level of needs, maintenance of the lower needs will continue to be a concern, even if not a verbalized one. Also, in a country where anyone can grow up to be president, it is only natural to peek at the next higher level of needs, to prepare to be ready when current needs are under control.

Looking at a program combining recognition, gratitude, and celebration in the context of Maslow's hierarchy brings order to what might otherwise appear to be a random collection of events, material, and procedures. It also explains why so many top executives feel that the satisfaction of controlling your own work environment, of knowing that you are doing a better job, should be reward enough. For them, it is.

Someone earning a six-figure income has his or her lower-level needs under firm control. The maintenance has been set in place and is rarely given a thought. It is also a good bet that their needs in belongingness and social areas are also well met through established procedures and networks. They are concentrating on fulfilling autonomy, self-esteem, and self-actualization needs. Self-actualization can be achieved, at least in part, by being able to control the elements of one's job, by making distinctive, personalized adjustments to how things are done. For a corporate vice-president that is thanks enough.

While a quality process will give people who have never had it before a chance to influence work conditions, it alone will not satisfy all of them. But throw in a mantle clock...

Does that make them ungrateful wretches? Shouldn't virtue be its own reward? No. A parallel example will help to illustrate the point. In 1975, following the collapse of South Vietnam, thousands of refugees flew out of Vietnam or were plucked out of boats by the U.S. Navy. Within days, some found themselves in a refugee camp in Camp Pendleton, California with no clothing beyond what they had been wearing when they left their semitropical homeland.

California in early May is cool (well, some say it is always cool, but in early May the temperature does not get very high), particularly in hills within reach of ocean breezes. To provide warmth, the Marine Corps issued to each refugee the one coat it had in stock—the standard olive-drab field jacket. The field jacket is clumsy, it is ugly, and, for most Vietnamese, it is oversized. But for people whose focus is on the first level of needs in the Maslow hierarchy (i.e., physiological—housing, clothing, food, etc.), the field jackets were just fine.

About two months later, Sears provided thousands of jackets in a variety of colors and sizes for the refugee camp. The idea was to trade the new jackets for the field jackets, thus allowing the Marine Corps to restock its shelves.

This time, the refugees who had been so grateful to get the ill-fitting, musty-smelling field jackets were suddenly very picky. The jacket exchange took many hours, as Vietnamese of both sexes and all ages tried on several different ones and modeled them for their friends. Many of the young Marines were quite upset at this radical change in attitude.

What had happened, of course, was that the level of the refugees' needs had changed. They were now confident that their physiological needs would be met, as well as the second-level needs, those of safety and security.

The new jackets were seen by the refugees in light of their needs for belongingness, and love, and autonomy and self-esteem. The Marines' frustration was caused by their failure to realize that not only do different people see things in different ways, but the same person will see the same things differently from time to time, depending on their personal set of circumstances.

It should not be surprising, then, that different employees will respond to different forms of gratitude. Nor can the perception of a particular person be predicted with any certainty. Two people earning exactly the same salary, and with objectively similar life styles and spending habits, may not be at the same level of needs—depending on their ambitions and expectations. One person who is, for example, a supervisor, may be thrilled to have risen so high. The person at the next desk, drawing the same salary, may be broken-hearted about being stuck as a supervisor. Since people normally try to fulfill Maslow's hierarchy of needs in a sequential manner, the first individual may be working on higher-level needs (level 4 or 5), while the latter is unhappy because they still do not feel secure, a level-2 need.

Applying the Principles

Just as it is true that no one approach will motivate every employee, it is equally true that there is no single correct approach. This gives a company a great deal of flexibility in designing its program.

Two points mitigate against a need to puzzle about why the employees—at any level—are putting forth ideas and taking part in a quality process. Initially, prizes and material items serve as a tangible pledge that the company is indeed serious about their quality effort. But as the habits of quality become ingrained and the new corporate culture touches more and more people, the prime motivation will change.

The other point is: who cares? If the star player on a basketball team sinks two free throws with no time left on the clock to win the big game, does anyone really care why he or she did it? Whether there was a bonus offered or the player did it for mom in the bleachers, what counts is that the team won. The team is better for the individual's efforts.

So it is with an employee in a quality process. Every quality idea, conceived or implemented, moves the team and the company a little further down the path to quality. Individual motives would be interesting for a psychological study but have little practical importance as long as the actions are taking place and a hospitable atmosphere for quality is being built and maintained. Form can precede content.

The key lies in having a widely, perhaps wildly, varied package. Rothchild Venture's Arch McGill's oft-quoted assertion that "the customer perceives service in his or her own terms" can easily and accurately be modified to "the employee perceives gratitude in his or her own terms."

Important, too, and worth repeating, is that what is described and recommended in this chapter is *not* an incentive program. It is a program based on gratitude and recognition. The difference is not simply a chicken and egg, which came first game of semantics. The prizes and publicity are given because they are deserved, and the company feels it appropriate and important to say thank you.

The Paul Revere is not unique in looking for expanded means of expressing gratitude to its employees. Even though pure quality circles disavow any individual rewards, allowing only symbolic awards such as certificates for the teams as a whole, some companies have enlarged their award programs. At McDonald Aircraft Company in St. Louis, for example, the 1985 recognition program for their quality circles includes:

- A merchandise award system developed by Maritz Motivation Co., the largest incentive company in the country. A customized gift catalog will feature more than 600 quality items.

- Dinners at first-rate local restaurants for new circles.
- Customized awards and group travel awards for members of top circles of the year and their spouses. These awards replace circle and team of the year awards.

McDonald Aircraft still uses the word "incentive," which implies a monetary view of motivation. The Paul Revere views the prizes and material items described in the pages that follow as tokens of gratitude. Quite clearly, they are not fair-value payment for the work being done. The company that believes its employees' enthusiasm can be bought with toaster ovens has some other problems to solve before starting a quality process. People just do not change their work habits and become enthusiastic practitioners of quality because they will get a fifty dollar item. They will, however, willingly work, and do exceptional work, for a company that expresses its gratitude for their efforts—even if the most expensive symbol of that gratitude is a fifty dollar item.

Gratitude and recognition make a potent combination. Recognition in the form of an article in a company publication may satisfy any of several needs, depending on the individual who is lauded in the story. An employee new to his or her position, or to the company for that matter, may be made to feel far more secure. "They won't fire me," the conscious or subconscious reasoning goes, "not while they're saying such good things about me."

Additionally, a story in the in-house paper may, if you are sure of your job but not of your relationship with your peers, help level-3 needs, particularly if a coworker says, "Hey, I saw the write-up. Nice job!"

Then, too, to people secure in their place among their peers and with no immediate fears of joining the ranks of the unemployed, a story in the paper might serve to reinforce their own self-image, their self-esteem. A public affirmation of one's worth (also known colloquially as a "public stroke") cannot help but legitimize and strengthen one's own feelings of worth. In short, it is nice to be told you are doing something right and that the company appreciates it.

For someone whose concentration is on self-actualization, the highest level of needs, a printed description of a particular accomplishment will reinforce that person's judgment that the action being taken does, in fact, coincide with the best interests of the company and should be continued.

Saying thank you in many different ways is an act of leadership. As long as a company insists on including human beings on its payroll, saying thank you will be necessary if superior performance is to be sustained. Since the program presented here is multifaceted, it is a fair bet that the message will get through. For some, the thank you will be heard in the gift; for some, it will come in the presentation of the gift; and, for still others, it will come in the publicity announcing the award of the gift. For many people all of these aspects count, albeit to different degrees for different individuals.

Setting the Standards

A recognition/gratitude/celebration scheme was one of the last aspects of the Quality Has Value process to be considered, due to the quality circle theory that awards should be tokens, if given at all. The first proposal was to split a defined percentage of the increase in profits with the employees. The idea was that a goal would be set for profit increase and that a given percentage of anything over that amount would be divided evenly among all the employees. The mail clerks would get the same bonus as the president.

The analogy to baseball salaries was offered. During the season, each player is paid according to his anticipated value to the team, so the all-star shortstop, for instance, gets quite a bit more than the player on the bench. If you make it to the World Series, however, the system changes. The pot of extra money is split into equal shares, and the star and the sub get the same size check.

However this plan ran afoul of corporate policy and presented anticipated difficulties, both in making fair estimates in advance of the impact of the quality process and in calculation and distribution of the funds. The decision was to proceed, instead, with a system with far more immediate rewards and with the focus on the Quality Teams rather than the company as a whole. The fact that 1984 was an Olympic year obviously influenced the terminology of the final plan, since the three categories defined were bronze, silver, and gold.

The plan was that as a team reached predetermined levels of achievement, they would receive certain material signs of gratitude for their efforts. The levels were:

Ten certified ideas or $10,000 in annualized savings = bronze

Twenty-five certified ideas or $25,000 in annualized savings = silver

Fifty certified ideas or $50,000 in annualized savings = gold

At the bronze level, each member of the team would receive a bronze-colored lapel pin. At silver, the physical gifts would be a silver pin and a gift from a prize catalog (items cost the company about twenty dollars each). A gold pin and a different catalog (fifty dollar items) awaited gold teams.

When the idea of lapel pins was first introduced, a member of the Quality Steering Committee remarked, "Nobody will wear them." The response from the former Marine who had made the suggestion was, "I just came out of twenty years in an organization where people risk their lives for little pieces of ribbon. Believe me, people will wear decorations that have meaning and value attached to them." Commercial firms designed the pins shown in Figure 5-1.

Honesty dictates acknowledgment that the bronze-silver-gold scheme was not based on careful research. The cutoff points were picked based on a combination of gut feeling and good guess. Making twenty-five the standard for silver and fifty the standard for gold had a nice symmetry to it, since it was the same as wedding anniversaries and would help to carry the scheme into post-Olympic years.

As mentioned in the last chapter, the average quality circle in America implements six ideas a year, while in Japan the average is between four and five. This was not discovered until after deciding on the goals of fifty, twenty-five and ten. Had it been known earlier, the Quality Team sights would most likely have been set a good bit lower. One of the stated criteria of the system, after all, was to put success within reach of everyone. Setting the lowest level of achievement at

Here's how the Quality Recognition Program works...

Bronze Award
When a team meets the qualification criteria for the Bronze Award, each team member receives a Bronze cloisonne lapel pin which recognizes each team member's contributions to "Paul Revere Quality."

Silver Award
When a Quality Team reaches the Silver Award level, each team member receives a Silver-plated lapel pin to show off his or her pride in Paul Revere Quality. In addition, each Silver Award qualifier receives the opportunity to select a merchandise award from an attractive selection of items from the Quality Awards Catalog J.

Gold Award
When a Quality Team reaches the Gold Award level, each team member receives a Gold-plated lapel pin...Paul Revere Quality at its best! In addition, each team member can select a merchandise award from the Quality Award Catalog F, which features a beautiful array of appealing items.

Figure 5-1. Quality Pins—1984

167 percent of the national average and the highest at 833 percent was, in retrospect, risky—or lucky. Lucky because the goals did turn out to be reachable by nearly everyone, although not without a great deal of hard work.

Allowing Quality Teams to reach the goals either through number of ideas or through money saved served two purposes. First, it made it attractive for teams to do the little things that count, although they were ideas that did not have an easily measurable monetary worth. This turned out to be one of the greatest assets of the Quality Has Value process, because it improved the working conditions of the teams and the customers' perception of the company's quality. Second, it allowed those teams that were not in areas controlling sizeable cash flows to compete on near-even terms with those that were. Both of these factors helped to reinforce the idea that quality was, indeed, the goal rather than just saving money.

It was not, of course, a surprise that improving the quality of the organization saved a great deal of money and produced increased income. The decision to institute the Quality Has Value process had been a business decision; it was made with the expectation that better quality meant better business. But the focus was clearly on quality.

This point was further reinforced when some of the quality improvements actually cost money. In those cases, for recognition purposes the value of the idea was set at zero, but since number of ideas was also counted, the team got full credit. Since quality remained the objective, a team was not denied the company's gratitude because in a particular instance the achievement of quality required investment.

The Paul Revere system fits one of the recommendations of the *Reward Systems and Productivity Final Report* for the White House Conference on Productivity: "Rewards systems should be based on measures of productivity, quality and other indicators of organizational health in addition to the traditional reliance on measures of financial performance."

Rewarding Success

Another major key to the success of The Paul Revere approach is the promptness of the reaction, that is, the short time between accomplishment and official recognition. According to the National Association of Suggestion Systems statistics, it took an average of 160 days in 1984 to implement an idea submitted through a standard suggestion system in American business. Any gratitude is then so far removed from the moment of inspiration that it is extremely difficult to build any momentum.

With Quality Team Central striving to certify all ideas within a week of being notified of their implementation and the cochairmen of the quality steering committee doing near-weekly rounds to say thank you momentum is maintained. Not only was the gratitude quick, the intent was to make it personal. Bronze, silver, and gold award ceremonies were carefully orchestrated. The two senior vice-presidents who were the Co-chairmen of the Quality Steering Committee each gave one or two hours per week to these presentations, averaging six bronze or silver awards a week in 1984. At a scheduled time, they would arrive at the work area of the team that had achieved either bronze or silver status. They would first talk with the team about what they had accomplished and emphasize the goals of the Quality Has Value process. Then pins and awards were presented.

The occasions were light, rather than somber, casual rather than formal. Doing it on the team's turf helped put the team members at ease. Handshakes and a personal thank you or congratulations for each team member were a natural part of the proceedings.

Interestingly, many employees at the lower rungs of the corporate ladder admitted to being surprised at how important the personal touch was. People who would perhaps be expected to place almost exclusive emphasis on the material gifts—who had openly proclaimed, "I'm doing this for the prizes"—found that having an executive come to them, ask them about their efforts, and thank them, greatly enhanced the value of the physical prize.

At the other end of the pay scale, a mirror reaction occurred. Men and women who had gone on record with their disdain of a system that gave radios admitted to being surprised at how pleased they were to arrive home and have their UPS-delivered gift waiting for them. Very often, if not every time, when they see or use it, they think warmly of the company that said thank you. To their surprise. It may not have met the level of need that is central to their life, but maintenance of lower level needs is always welcome.

Also interesting, the quality pins did become an everyday piece of jewelry for many employees. To boost the percentage of pin wearers, a lunch-for-a-pin program was created. Once a week, a member of Quality Team Central would pick ten names out of a hat that contained all the names of the employees in the Home Office. The Quality Team Central member would then go to each of the ten people, and, if the employee had a quality pin on, he or she would receive a free lunch pass.

Some employees wore the pins just on the chance of getting a free lunch, at least initially. Others wore them because it enhanced their feeling of belongingness. Still others wore them as a mark of pride, a matter of self-esteem. Whatever the reason, the pins were worn, and they served as a constant reminder of the quality process. The pins also served as instruments of peer pressure, and then pressure on the management level, since management teams tended to lag behind those led by supervisors and below.

When a Quality Team made it to the gold status with fifty ideas or $50,000 in savings, the presentation routine changed a bit. The seventy-two gold teams in 1984 received a visit from the company President—and the photographer. The president was to mark the occasion; the photographer was to record it for the company newspaper.

Once the process was under way, every issue of *The Lantern* included pictures of gold teams, along with a listing of some of their more noteworthy ideas. *The Lantern*, however, had other news to print as well as 2,500 employees scattered throughout the country who needed to be informed about the company. A vehicle was needed to recognize and celebrate more than just gold teams and to present ideas about the many facets of quality.

To fill the need, *Quality News* was born as a monthly, one page, two sided, "good time news" newsletter. Whenever a team made it to the bronze level, the names of all members of the team appeared in the next issue of *Quality News*; the names of silver teams were listed; and the gold team names, with the name of the team leader, made it onto the front page (See Figure 5-2).

Quality News was intended to tell the employees about the positive things, the quality things, that their co-workers were doing. In addition, stories that told about quality aspects of the company that may have moved into the taken-for-granted category were included as were ideas about quality that might help in understanding this surprisingly complex and all-pervasive concept. But mostly *Quality News* became a vehicle for recognition and celebration, for publicly applauding a team's or an individual's efforts.

Adding Variety

When the bronze-silver-gold scheme was first defined, it was not envisioned as a major time commitment for top management. A few teams, it was reasoned, would no doubt make it to gold late in the year—maybe by September or maybe by October. The first team made it to gold on the strength of fifty ideas certified by early April, after only twelve weeks. At their award ceremony they asked, half-jokingly, "What's next?" so, the categories were increased.

Double gold was defined as fifty more certified ideas or $50,000 more in annualized savings. Upon achieving the gold level, a team's counters were reset to zero, meaning that if they made it to gold based on one big idea worth more than $50,000, they now needed another $50,000 to reach double gold. When a team did attain the newly described status, they would be allowed to choose another item from the gold catalog and would have lunch in the private dining room with one of the executives of the company and their bosses. The private dining room, incidentally, is used only for specific occasions and is available to any employees that want to use it.

One team did reach triple gold just before the fiscal year rushed to a close. All the team members received still another gift from the catalog, and one of the Co-chairmen of the Quality Steering Committee took them out to one of the fancier restaurants in town for a memorable lunch.

Other attempts to add variety to the program were sought. Inventing occasions to celebrate the accomplishments—large and small—of employees adds spice to any recognition/gratitude program. There should be major overhauls introduced on an annual or biannual basis, but short-term variations can be thrown in on an irregular basis. These can be small, enjoyable things the only purpose of which is to make some employees a little bit happier about their efforts or to focus attention on the quality process.

This idea is simple. Offer to trade some small token of gratitude (e.g., a free lunch at the company cafeteria, assuming that is not perceived as a punishment or a cactus, so the employee can be "Stuck on Quality") for a copy of any letter or note received by an employee thanking them for something they have done.

The only real decision to be made is whether or not to limit the program to thank you letters that come from outside the organization. The advantage of including intracompany letters of gratitude in the offer is that it reinforces the concept of a customer being *anyone* to whom a product, service, or information is provided—including the person at the next desk.

The disadvantage is that there will be cases of people writing to each other and then having a free lunch together. The price of two lunches is, however, a small price to pay for (1) encouraging everyone to express their appreciation (it may get to be a habit) and (2) displaying trust in the employees to present only earned letters as trade-ins for the defined recognition.

Criteria for accepting letters must be generous, and the trade must be completed quickly and easily. Parts of the letters can then be used in *Quality News*. Examples of some received and traded for free lunches were:

> "I would like to express my gratitude for the timely response."
> "I want to thank you so much for taking care of the tree on my property, which fell last week.... Paul Revere has always been a good neighbor to me."
> "Thank you again for your time and your valuable advice."
> "I just want to thank you for your help in this entire mess for which I am totally ashamed."

These letters-for-a-lunch (or, during one month, letters-for-a-dictionary) were run every several months, whenever it seemed as though a pick-me-up was needed. They complemented

QUALITY NEWS

The Paul Revere Companies
Our policy is quality.

The Actuaries-A Quality Division

Long range projects which will result in permanent increases in the Quality of their work have been the goal of the Actuarial Division's Quality Teams.

The five division teams have concentrated their efforts on devising methods to insure professionalism throughout. By analyzing training needs — initial and refresher — and taking a hard look at their people and their products, they feel they have made giant strides toward becoming a truly Quality division.

Lois Bizak heads up the Corporate Actuarial team, the *Terminally Reserved*. In order to improve their training, they have developed a notebook for newly hired members of their staff. It contains company information, corporate actuarial administration information, and work aids. It is now going to print, will be given to everyone in corporate and product actuarial, and will become part of the regular development program.

They have also assembled a ½" thick "Corporate Actuarial Training Program Reading Material" book which will be of particular use to actuarial trainees. Lois states that she is "really pleased with the fact that they identified the thing that they felt was really important, even though it was long range."

Dick Mucci and the *A Prime Team* represent Product Actuarial. The primary force of their Quality meetings has been the updating of the User Developed Systems manual. The primary workers have been Rick Farrell, Al Riggieri, and Paul Weaver.

Since approximately half of an actuarial student's time is spent with a computer, this effort will make sure that that time is far more efficient and thus improve the Quality of the entire Division.

Their other big project is an attempt to improve the accuracy of data in the Group Statistical Systems. With an estimated worth of over $100,000, this is being pursued in cooperation with Quality Teams *Just Us* (Norm Clark) and *D-T-N-M Savers* (Debbie Kalvinek).

Working with the *A Prime Team* on the UDS manual are Dave Libbey and his team from Life and Health Product Actuarial. In fact Al Riggieri, a member of the Task Force, is on Dave's team. *(Continued on back)*

AUGUST GOLD TEAMS: Charlie Sanders and *Navigators*, Warren Bock and *DI-Namics*, Bella Hickey and *Bella's Bombers*, Barbara Kempski and *NBC Team*, Christine Richards and *Local 440's*, Lou Jacques and *Tech Services*, and Lauren Knapik and *Rat Patrol*.

Double Gold!

"We started like everyone else and when we reached the first Gold, I figured there would be a big letdown but the ideas just kept coming. Then we got close to Double Gold and they decided to be the first." Phyl Scully and her *Scullywags* were indeed the first Double Gold Paul Revere Quality Team — achieving the status through 100 certified ideas.

What next? Phyl says, "We've got six more ideas on the system so they will be on their way again. Up to now they have been looking at their own jobs — what they do, how they do it, whether or not the should continue to do it. Now I want to get into more difficult ideas that directly affect our customers."

The current members of the *Scullywags* are Phyl Scully, Nancy Lucier, Virginia McCallum, Roberta Stowe, Evelyn Johnson, Nancy Oleszewski, Beverly Yvanauskas, Janice Strout, Brendalee Lemieux, Pat Bigeau, Kim Anderson, and Carol Bigelow.

Model Employee

Joan Hurley, whose team *The Deadliners* was the first Gold team, is going to be in a magazine advertisement for the Zenger Miller Group Action program.

On Friday, August 24, she flew to New York for a photo and interview session. Her hour and a half in front of the camera (120 pictures) and half hour interview were accompanied by fresh fruit, wine, and generally first-class treatment.

Thanks to the efforts of people like Joan, The Paul Revere is becoming well known for its Quality.

Quality = Enjoyment

"They that are serious in ridiculous things will be ridiculous in serious things" — Cato the Elder

One of the greatest strengths of the Quality Has Value process is that it provides us all with a vehicle to insure that our priorities are straight. Better yet, if we shed ourselves of unnecessary chores and procedures, our jobs can't help but be more fun.

Humor should be a natural part of the work place — ranging from the quiet enjoyment which comes from doing a job well to loud laughter at the genuinely funny things that happen from time to time.

Satisfaction and enjoyment... two of the inherent goals of The Paul Revere's Quality Has Value process.

Figure 5-2. Quality News

ISP — The Quality of Life

In August 1980, when the ISP began, there was no similar savings program available to Paul Revere employees. On June 30, 1984, the total value of Paul Revere employee accounts was over $8 million dollars, including contributions made to employee accounts by the company. There are now more than 1,000 active Paul Revere Participants, and the "average" Paul Revere account has a value of over $7,000.

Here's how the plan can work for you. Suppose your REGULAR contributions are $100 a month. With Paul Revere's 50% match and assuming investment earnings of 9%, your account would grow to almost $250,000 after 30 years. (Of course if investment earnings are higher or lower than 9%, this amount will vary.) The current rate of interest paid on Fund C (Fixed income fund) is 14%.

The Paul Revere . . . working to improve the Quality of Life.

The Actuaries — A Quality Division Continued

The Wizards are also using the task force approach to enable work on several long range projects simultaneously. Dave states that their aim is to get "new and better products on the street quicker."

Diane Grindley and the *Class Acts* make up the Actuarial Service Unit. They are transferring several large activities onto the Personal Computers in their area, believing that the large initial time investment will be well worth it in the long run.

They are also working on a "5-level development tree" to let their people know exactly what steps must be accomplished to make career progressions.

Diane frequently turns over functional leadership of the team meetings to Susan Perron.

The Division Head, John Knutson, leads the *Q team* and is very proud of his division's accomplishments to date — and those of his own team. They have just completed a "development tree" which spells out the "profile of skills that a professional actuary ought to have and details the formal training, work, and experience they should undergo to develop those skills."

The plan is currently "to the division for comments" and should be in place by the end of the month. John's assessment: "It's going to be dynamite. It will create Quality in the division, pride in the outfit, and pride in themselves."

The Actuarial Division — preparing to be Quality for a long, long time.

Names of Bronze Team Members

KEN'S KOST KONTROLLERS: Ken McNulty, Deke Bardsley, Barb Harper, Bob Howard, Ray Kingman, Pat Morris, Shirley Salah, Dave Strieby. **TOOTH FAIRIES:** Debbie Sanders, Sandy Skrzek, Donna Naumiec, Lisa DesChamps. **Q-TIPS:** Bob Edgar, Betty Swisher, Janet Falvey, Mark Babayon, Pete Spence, Diane O'Brien. **TITANS OF COMMERCE:** R. P. Deal, Jean Quinn, Bill Gaffney, Dr. Harry Kramer, Dick Robbins, Dave Keenan, Ken Blood, Carroll Smith. **BLUE KNIGHTS:** Paul Jette, Joe Zuromsky, George Lindstrom, Allan Andre, Lisa Andre, Dot Clouthier, Kenneth Gaucher, Dick Grann, Russ Harman, Dick Hebert, Dick Hillman, Bob Jobin, Paul Koulisis, Bobby Lewis, Bob Maramo, Lucien Mercure, Erv Osganian, John Pantos, Tom Phouthavong, Diana Picotte, Bob Picotte, Bill Rizzuti. **COLLECTION GIRLS:** Nancy Nettelbladt, Christine Rice, Isabel McKinlay, Pat DiCisare, Pam Hohne, Carolyn Smith, Connie Wrightson, Vicky Faint. **JAN'S JEMS:** Janet Pasquale, Brenda Jenkins, Sandra Westerberg, Nancy Cote, Bridget McKinnon, Margaret McCart, Therese Trudeau, Joan Cowee, Angela Stumbras, Dorothy Miron, Bonnie Thomas, Judy Gagnon, Beth Tetreault. **COMMUNIGATORS:** Bob Jeffrey, Chuck Dubois, Carol Malysz, Joan Wackell, Al Lemire, Lauren Knapik. **BUG REPELLERS:** Wink Langston, Jim Alexander, Win Shute, Pete Smith, Ken Spence.

Figure 5-2. (continued)

Teachers of Quality

The Paul Revere is not alone in its desire to become a Quality company. Our Quality Has Value process is unique but the avalanche of advertisers exclaiming their "quality" shows that others have the same goal.

The two most visible apostles of this Quality Revolution in America are Thomas J. Peters and W. Edwards Deming. While both have the same basic message, i.e., that Quality can and should be attained and maintained, they are widely divergent in their approaches.

Deming's reputation was made in Japan where he taught statistical Quality Control to the shattered post-World War II industries. He wasn't well known in this country until a 1980 TV documentary. His emphasis is on numbers and physical measurements, and on insisting that workers can, with good management and good machinery, produce goods well within Quality-defining tolerances.

Peters' fame came as a result of the message in the book "In Search of Excellence", which he co-authored with Robert Waterman. They too proclaimed Quality as the goal but their approach was to describe what they had found to be consistent in the operations of 43 successful, excellent American companies.

In his subsequent lectures (and now the Toward Excellence video/text course which is offered here at The Paul Revere), Peters has repeatedly stressed that it is the people who work in an organization — at all levels — who make the difference. "Sure," he says, "statistical quality control is important IF the attitude of the people is right."

Peters and Deming have, it appears, opposing assessments of the current state of American management. Deming says, "The one thing we must never export is American management — at least not to friendly countries." Peters, on the other hand, feels that there are numerous examples of good American management and, through the Toward Excellence program is, indeed, exporting it.

The two do agree on one crucial point — the importance of the customer. Deming has said, "Who can put a price on a satisfied customer and who can figure out the cost of a dissatisfied customer?" Peters numbers "Existing for the Customer" among his five fundamentals for achieving excellence.

It is this emphasis on the customer — inside and outside of the company — that is making The Paul Revere a truly Quality organization.

#100

The *Q-Tips*, led by Bob Edgar were The Paul Revere's 100th Bronze Team! Appropriately enough, they made it both ways — with 10 certified ideas worth over $14,000. Congratulations to Bob and the Century Bronze Team.

August Silver Teams

Gold Panthers, Petit's Pussycats, Titans of Commerce.

September 1, 1984

the weekly pin-for-a-lunch program. During the summer months of 1985, when ideas began to lag, a month-of-sundaes program was used to spur activity. Any team that had ten ideas or $10,000 certified during the month of August received certificates for sundaes in The Paul Revere cafeteria. A total of fifty three teams took advantage of the offer, implementing ideas worth over $1 million.

Celebrating: Don't Forget to Party

The idea of celebration was deliberately built into the recognition/gratitude/celebration program. Its purpose was to serve as a reminder that work can be a source of pleasure, enjoyment, and fun. In too many businesses, a smile is seen as either a sign of incipient simple-mindedness or proof that the smiler is not working very hard. Fun and work are considered to be mutually exclusive.

The opposite, of course, should be the case. Holding on to your employees is an important consideration to all employers—both to build expertise within the company and to reduce training costs. Yet, how can an employee be expected to stay in a job that he or she does not enjoy and to work hard in it as well? A sense of enjoyment goes a long way toward involving employees in a movement toward quality. It is not optional.

The tone was set at the official beginning of the Quality Team process on January 13, 1984. Both to add weight to the occasion and because of a shortage of large meeting rooms in The Paul Revere Home Office building, the kickoff was held at Mechanics Hall, a magnificently restored nineteenth-century music hall located only a block away from the Home Office. In addition to the Great Hall, there are meeting rooms of various sizes, and it was one of these that was rented for the Friday the thirteenth kickoff.

The enrollees in the then ongoing Quality Team leader course were invited, as were the Quality Steering Committee members and the company president. The meeting began with a series of rather standard (read unexciting) presentations about the process that was about to begin.

Unknown to the team leaders, however, on the afternoon before a piece of foolishness had been planned. The Quality Team Tracking Program had been available on the computers throughout the building for almost two weeks. A few dozen team leaders had received training on how to use the system, and twelve of them had logged at least one idea onto it. Near the end of the hour-long meeting, these twelve were called to the front of the room with no explanation. Once they were lined up, their pace-setting actions were announced. On a signal, a gorilla with a load of balloons burst into the room, hopped to the front, and handed balloons to the bemused team leaders while flashbulbs popped. After chasing the photographer for a bit, the gorilla bounded out of the room, but not before he handed a balloon to the company president who, after his opening remarks, had sat down in the audience. The sight of this tall, gray, and distinguished New England gentleman with his balloon was a wonderful signal to all the team leaders of his commitment to the process, his willingness to be involved personally, and showed that everyone could have some fun along the way.

It seemed appropriate, if not essential, that the completion of the first year of the Quality Has Value process be marked by some similar event. The answer was the Quality Celebration. The idea was to provide both an appropriate setting for the announcement of the Most Valuable Player (MVP) and the Most Valuable Team (MVT) winners and runners-up and to thank the entire work force for their surprisingly enthusiastic acceptance of and involvement in the whole Quality Has Value process.

A return to Mechanics Hall was decided upon, but this time the Great Hall was chosen. The stage that had once welcomed such celebrities as Charles Dickens would now be the scene of an unabashed celebration.

Picking the MVP and MVT was, naturally, the first step. The idea for MVP and MVT grew out of discussions in the Quality Steering Committee meetings in late 1983. The Paul Revere had had a suggestion system, as was mentioned earlier, and it was considered to be a successful one. In 1983, there were 216 suggestions submitted, with 86 implemented, resulting in a savings of $41,000. Using 25 percent of first-year savings as the rule for awards to individuals and, on several occasions, 25 percent to the section that implemented the idea, the program had resulted in the distribution of just over $12,000 in cash prizes. Since the company was dropping this system with its potential for big money, even if seldom earned, it was argued that the company was in danger of looking cheap. After all, the only material awards were a pin and two gifts with a total value of seventy dollars.

Partially in answer to this concern, a plan for year-end winners was devised. Near the end of the fiscal year (November 30), nominations for MVP and MVT would be solicited. A purely objective system was impossible—quality both in fact and perception has too many subjective elements. All gold teams or teams that expected to make gold before November 30 (there were seventy two gold teams the first year) were invited to nominate themselves for MVT and one or more of their members for MVP. The provision for one or more was included to avoid a division within a team over which of several enthusiastic people to nominate.

The forms were kept simple, both to make nominating easier and to keep scoring as straightforward as possible. When the nominations were received at Quality Team Central, each of the eight members of the Quality Steering Committee was given a complete set. They were asked to score them and return them to Quality Team Central. The top ten in each category were then decided upon, and smaller packages of nominations were distributed to the president of the company and his six-member staff for another round of scoring.

While the scoring/placing of any one individual was subjective, the assumption was that the sum of all these subjective ratings, gut reactions, and best guesses would give as objective a result as possible or at least as fair a result as possible. Fortunately, the consistency of the final choices appeared to support that theory.

The results were held secret, within reason. The person dealing with the trophy and plague engravers, for instance, was informed and sworn to secrecy. The *Quality News* issue that would normally have been published on December 1 was not printed until the morning of the Quality Celebration, December 5, so that it could be distributed the same afternoon and include the names of the winners.

The Great Hall holds 1,350 people, more than enough room for the entire Home Office work force. The Quality Celebration was the first time in anyone's memory that all the Home Office employees were gathered at one time, perhaps since the company's founding in 1895.

The awards were announced by a co-chairman of the Quality Steering Committee and handed out by the President of The Paul Revere and the Chairman of the Board of AVCO.

All team members who were nominated for MVP (not just the top ten) won at least $100. Those who did not make the top five were announced, stood and received the applause of their fellow employees, and were given their check. The four runners-up each received a check for $250 and an engraved Paul Revere bowl. The MVP received a check for $1,000 and a Paul Revere bowl big enough to hold the contents of at least two bottles of champagne.

To stress the importance of team activity, the MVT awards were given after the MVP presentations. Four teams were designated as runners-up, with each team member receiving a check for $100 and a plaque. The MVT—the team that had been the first to reach the gold level and had gone on to double gold—members received $500 apiece and Paul Revere bowls. The theme music from *Chariots of Fire* provided the background to their dancing, jubilant run onto the stage.

Every member of the audience was given their own surprise. They got the rest of the day off—a popular decision. They got a choice of a ham or turkey for Christmas and a costumed Minuteman handed them each a balloon with the logo AVCO-Paul Revere-Quality as they left.

As 1985 unfolded, many team leaders pointed to the Quality Celebration as the reason why their particular team, and the quality process in general, accelerated going into its second year. They *knew* success was possible, that they were not alone in their efforts to improve quality, and that the company would say thank you in a way that they understood.

Launching a Second Year

For 1985, the recognition/gratitude program was adjusted to reflect some of the lessons learned. The quality pins, for instance, were redesigned, but not because the 1984 design was unsatisfactory or because it was believed that people enjoyed amassing a collection of lapel pins. Rather, the change was precipitated because many of the female employees did not like sticking the pseudo-tie tacks through their garments. As a result, more than a few had missed a free lunch because they had chosen not to wear their pin on the day when their name had been picked. The 1985 pins were designed to come in two styles—tie tack with the push-through post and clutch and charm with a small loop for hanging from a necklace or bracelet. The percentage of female employees wearing their quality pins immediately rose, resulting in that many more reminders to everyone about quality—and more free lunches.

The biggest change was in the distribution of gifts given to the members of teams as they progressed through the bronze-silver-gold hierarchy. Instead of a gift catalog, gift certificates were used—Paul Revere gift certificates. Achieving the bronze level now resulted in each team member receiving one ten dollar certificate, the silver level meant two certificates, and gold brought four more ten dollar certificates. With this method, all employees would be able to meet their own needs. Basic needs or social needs could be met at the discretion of the employees whenever they wanted to use the certificates.

The businesses that accepted the certificates ranged from a popular discount/general merchandise store to exclusive clothing boutiques to elegant eateries. Before the first ones were issued, members of Quality Team Central lined up twenty two stores and restaurants that would accept the new "funny money." As the year progressed, more and more stores were added to the list—some contacted at the request of employees and some because they approached Paul Revere or simply accepted the certificates and sent them in for reimbursement.

One side benefit was the enhancement of the company's standing in the business community. The effect was not unlike that achieved by various military bases in past years when, to remind a neighboring community of the economic ties between the base and community, all personnel would be paid in two-dollar bills. Filling cash registers all over town with two-dollar bills may not be the most subtle message, but it is a powerful one.

Not only did the gift certificates remind merchants of the impact of The Paul Revere payroll, it gave the employees endless opportunities to talk about quality and The Paul Revere Quality Has Value process.

Other changes in the recognition/gratitude program concerned the MVP and MVT awards. Monthly MVPs and MVTs would be chosen in 1985, with the reward centering on recognition. The team and individual would be picked by Quality Team Central and the Co-chairmen of the Quality Steering Committee, using as their criteria the year's stated objectives. The dual objectives for 1985 were set as improving the customer's perception of the company's quality and reducing the cost of nonconformance. The MVP and MVT would be those individuals and teams who had done the most to further these goals. They would be publicized in *Quality News* and would, of course, increase their chances for year-end honors.

The MVT of the month was given possession of a large banner to hang in their area for the month and the MVP received a small plaque proclaiming her or him the most valuable player of the month. Placing this plaque on the dashboard allowed the winner to park in the prime parking area closest to the building—an area normally limited to people with longevity at the company, regardless of pay level. Competition for MVP was exceptionally keen during the winter months.

The year-end procedures were also altered. The 1985 MVP and MVT awards were restructured to make the top prizes in each category equal. Additionally, by expanding the number of MVP winners, it was admitted that determining a single MVP was a particularly inexact science. In 1985, there was a ten-way tie for first place in the MVP competition, and a fifteen-way tie for runner-up. Each of the MVP's received $500 and a Paul Revere paperweight, while the runners-up each received $100 and a less elaborate paperweight. The awards for MVT were to parallel those of the MVPs. Each member of the MVT would receive $500 and a Paul Revere paperweight, while each of the four runner-up teams (no differentiation between second and fifth, just a four-way tie for second) would receive $100 and a less elaborate paperweight. Recognition of the year-end MVPs and MVTs through *The Lantern, Quality News*, and the Quality Celebration would be supplemented by a permanent trophy/plaque on display in the company cafeteria.

6

Change in Corporate Culture

Theory loses its value unless its validity is verified through implementation. It is relatively simple to decide to elicit quality ideas, but what are they? What is a quality idea worth? Must it have a dollar value? What if top management is willing to commit to quality but does not have a clear pattern of behavior in mind? These were among a host of questions that arose during the implementation of the Quality Has Value process.

The next two chapters will be devoted to a description of the process in action at The Paul Revere Insurance Companies during 1984 and 1985. While there may not be one *correct* answer to any of the questions above, here are some answers that work. The intent is to present options and approaches that can either be copied wholesale or modified to fit a particular company's personality and circumstances. This chapter is divided into subtopics for easy reference.

Quality Ideas

At the time of the January 13, 1984 launching of the Quality Teams, Quality Team Central was, to put it kindly, unsettled about what their exact procedures would be, particularly with regard to the certification of ideas. Ideas that saved money were, by definition, quality ideas. But what constituted a quality idea besides saving money? A major problem with basing certification solely on monetary calculations was that this would raise the suspicion that the program was really just a money saving device after all. It took a lot of explanation and a lot of reassurance to convince employees that this was not the case.

Quality Team Central decided the keys to winning converts were common sense and generosity. It had been recommended to all team leaders that they devote the first two or three meetings to "messing around with quality," an exercise that had proved valuable to the Quality Steering Committee early in 1983. The intent was to discuss the concept of quality, to decide what it actually meant to the members of the team, and to begin to build a vocabulary with which to address the problems at hand more easily.

One of the first four gold teams, the Bookies, attributed their early success to having developed their own criteria for assessing tasks:

Does the work do what it is intended to do?

Is there a better way of doing it?

Is it repetitious?

Is it outdated?

Another team reported that they had simply decided to take "a look at the way we were doing things and had been doing things for ten to fifteen years. There had to be easier and better ways."

Once a team had some agreement as to what it was they were trying to accomplish, often the next meeting was devoted to a freewheeling brainstorming session. The idea was to develop a list of things that they would like to change. The challenge for the team leaders was to keep these meetings from being "bitch sessions" and to keep the team focused on solving problems.

This naturally suggested the question: did a quality idea solve a problem, whether it saved money or not? The answer was yes—money or no. This tied in with the definition of a problem. When some people examine the statistics of The Paul Revere in the first years of the Quality Has Value process, their reaction is "Those folks must really have been in rough shape if they could identify that many problems!" The Paul Revere was not in poor shape (it was, after all, a consistent moneymaker and a leader in its field); but yes, Quality Teams did identify that many problems. The word "problem," however, was used to define the area between where a person or unit is and where they could be—even if where they are is already pretty good. A problem, then, not only represented a move from bad to good; it also represented a move from good to better and then to better yet.

"But," the cynics countered, "what if a problem exists because of a failure on the part of the team itself? Should a team get credit for something they (or we) should have been doing all along?" The answer? Granted, perhaps it should have been done all along, but it wasn't, and now it is. If the team leader felt that the catalyst for the change from "should have been" to "is" was the quality process, then it was a quality idea. Perhaps this is generous, but it is also good common sense. Quality Team members were not yet absolutely sure of themselves; quick refusals based on artificially high standards would have been counterproductive.

Small ideas, therefore, were allowed, even encouraged, as long as it could be shown that the idea had been implemented and that it had a positive impact on the quality of the unit, in fact or in perception. Team leaders were urged to begin with a few small ideas to build momentum. Many teams received credit for things as simple and as small as moving a filing cabinet ten feet closer to the one person who has frequent use of it. A quality idea? Technically, perhaps not, but the inconvenient location of that cabinet most likely had been a matter of irritation fifteen times a day for the person who had to walk the extra dozen or so steps. Could it have been moved prior to the Quality Has Value process? Perhaps in theory it could have been, but the person being inconvenienced did not believe it or did not want to go through the hassle of asking permission through however many layers of management that it might have taken.

Small ideas served as small tests. After all, if a team could move a filing cabinet, could control that admittedly small piece of their environment, why not try something bigger? If not, why believe any of that stuff? And the person freed of the recurring annoyance might in fact be better able to concentrate on doing his or her job.

Even a list could be a quality idea. This one, put together by The Big Guys (the team that included the company president), was titled "Meeting Guidelines" and included:

> Need the meeting be held at all? Could the purpose be served through the attention and efforts of one or two people?
>
> Meetings should be used for problem solving and/or decision making, not for dissemination of information which can be handled by memorandum, telephone, etc.
>
> Publish on your agenda the estimated total cost of your meeting using an average cost per person for Home Office employees.
>
> No more than 25 percent of your time should be spent in meetings. If you are spending more, you may need better organization.
>
> I would suggest that it would be a good idea to eliminate all meetings on Fridays. This would give everyone an opportunity to end each week with as few unfinished tasks as possible. Hopefully, we could have *"Meetless" Fridays* throughout the company.

Many ideas did save money, about 60 percent of them. The monetary score-keeping device chosen by default was "annualized dollars"; it was the system that had been used in the old work measurement studies and was a familiar method. The approach assessed each idea, determined if it had any savings, and determined whether those savings would be one-time or continuous. If the latter, the savings per month were multiplied by twelve to determine the annualized savings. An idea implemented in October, therefore, became equal to one implemented in February if it saved the same number of hours by an employee at the same pay level.

A distinction was drawn between "hard" and "soft" dollars. Hard dollars consisted of either budgeted money that would not be spent or additional income that otherwise would not have been generated. Hard dollars were referred to as "money we could go to the bar and drink with." The soft dollar total was made up primarily of time or capacity savings. If a unit improved (or cancelled) a procedure and saved itself five hours a week, or 250 hours a year, it received credit toward recognition for $2,500 saved (assuming the person whose time had been saved earned ten dollars an hour, including benefits).

There were several possibilities for the time saved. One was increased capacity, that is, the unit could take on additional work; or someone might actually be able to do a quality job of what they were supposed to do now that an overload had been removed; or there might be a reduction in complement. This normally happened after several time-savings when someone left the department and the unit looked around and said, "You know, we've saved over 2,000 hours. If we just divvy up his (or her) duties, we won't have to replace them." At that point, the soft dollars became hard.

Calculating dollars was relatively straightforward. Other decisions were not so easily made. The opening weeks were mercifully slow (although seven teams did make it to the bronze level in the first five weeks), allowing the analysts and director to hold frequent conferences to decide how to handle specific cases and to generalize those decisions into guidelines.

One such suggestion: could credit be shared if an idea generated by one Quality Team required the cooperation of another team in order to be implemented? It was decided that if team A and team B cooperated on an idea, both would receive credit for an implemented idea. If there were any savings attached, they would be split between the teams, according to whatever percentage split the team leaders approved. If, however, team A had the idea, worked out the implementation, set it in motion, and thereby caused a change in the work procedures for the people in team B, did team B share the credit? This prompted another conference, another series of conversations with various team leaders, and another decision. In order to receive credit for sharing an idea, a team would have to be part of the formulation of the idea or part of the decision to implement the idea.

An even thornier question involved the amount of credit new or transferred team members had in relationship to their new teams. It was apparent that no formula would cover every case, so the Director—Quality Team Central decided to make a virtue of necessity. The policy was to trust the judgment of the team leaders, hoping that the example of generosity and common sense would prevail. It did. Team members who have left the company have received the same awards as their teammates when their contribution was judged to be significant.

It should be pointed out that the gradual start mentioned above was gradual only in comparison to what was to come. Compared to the average quality circle program, where the careful admonition is to not look for any results for the first several months, Quality Team Central was awash in ideas. By February 17, there were 1,385 ideas entered on the Quality Team Tracking Program, with 167 of those already implemented. Another admonition often heard with quality circles is that after an initial burst of enthusiasm and results activity often declines rapidly. The Quality Has Value process began with a comparative rush, hit a peak after about a year and a half, and has stayed at that peak.

The amazing growth rate for the first year of the Quality Has Value process, from the inauguration through November 1984 (the end of The Paul Revere fiscal year), is presented in Figure 6-1. It shows the monthly growth in implemented, certified ideas for the period. In June, eighteen teams achieved silver status; in October, seventeen teams reached gold status and six made it to the double gold level. Most teams earned recognition due to the number of ideas implemented, rather than because of money saved, although, in one happy coincidence, the one-hundredth team to qualify for bronze (the Q-Tips, in August) managed to exceed $10,000 in savings with their tenth idea.

In October 1 *Quality News*, a short article titled "A Look Back" read:

> One of the major lessons learned during the first year of the Quality Has Value process is the ability of the employees—at all levels—to think of ways to improve what management has thought for years were perfectly good procedures.
>
> A caution to all team leaders—never just dismiss an idea without giving your team a chance to discuss it. Experience has proven that the overwhelming majority of ideas proposed

Change in Corporate Culture 107

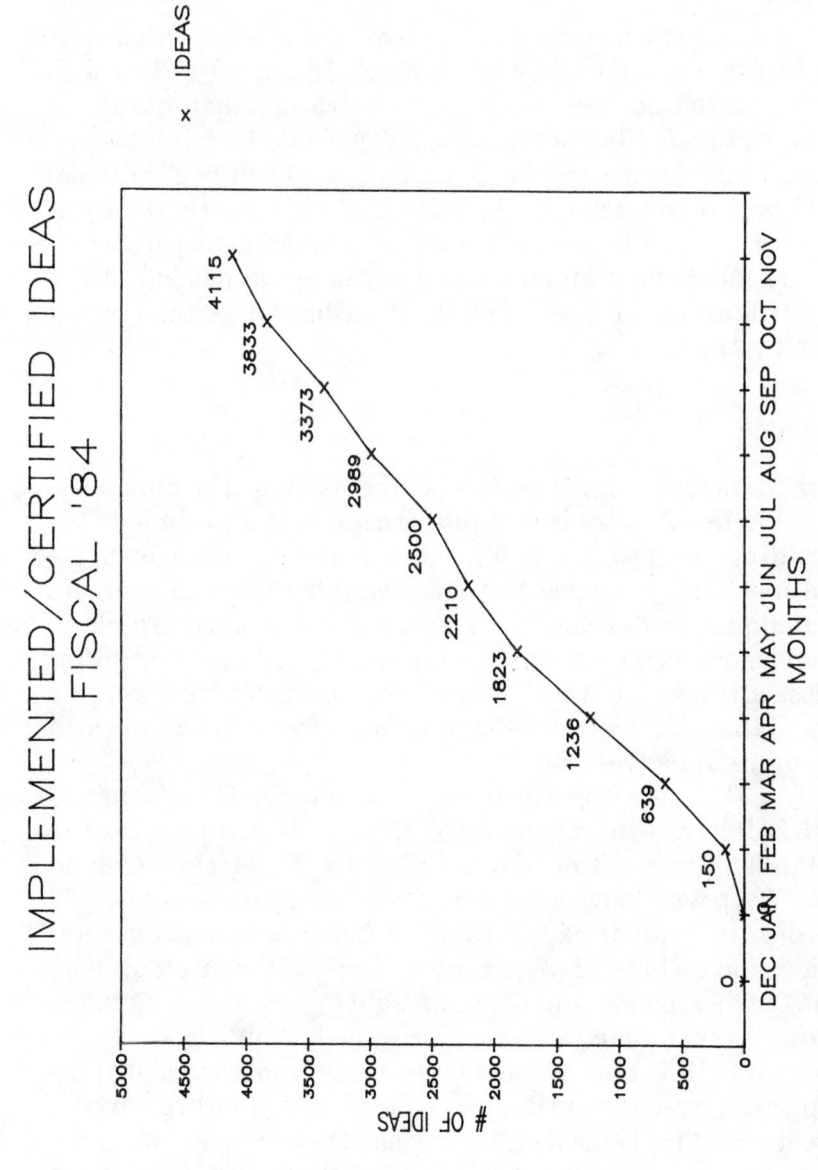

Figure 6-1. Quality Has Value 1984—Certified Ideas

have been good ones...or have, through discussion, led to good ones. Quality is everyone's business.

As is natural in any endeavor of this size, there were pockets of excellence, and there were pockets of disinterest. The decision was to take the easy approach—rather than harangue and harrass the laggards, the energy would be put into celebrating the front-runners. The Director—Quality Team Central would contact the team leaders of low-activity teams (almost always teams composed of management personnel) once a month or so and inquire if any help was needed; otherwise the approach was to pull the front end rather than trying to push the back end.

Training

Traditions take time to establish themselves. The announcement of the Quality Has Value process was a prelude to the building of new traditions and a change in corporate culture—and there was no time to wait for new management techniques to develop. The management goals were clear: demonstrate commitment to the quality process and foster those attitudes of creativity and independence that were its foundation. To deal with the practical aspects, it was decided to jumpstart a tradition.

The Program for Ensuring that Everybody's Thanked (PEET) began in the spring of 1984. This was the effort to establish the habit of Management by Wandering Around (MBWA), which everyone conceded was a wonderful idea in theory. Individual excuses for not being a practitioner are many and include: "I'm just not that type," "I'm just too busy," and "I tried it once, and nobody would tell me anything interesting." It can take years to reverse such thinking.

With PEET, the excuses were simply ignored. Each of the top seven executives (later expanded to fifteen) received a sheet (the "PEET sheet," what else?) each week with the names of two team leaders, their locations, and their phone numbers. It was the executive's responsibility to go to the person's area and talk with them. There was no set time, no set topic, although talking about quality rather than baseball was certainly one option to be considered. Recognizing the artificiality of the situation ("Here, executive A, go talk to supervisor B"), the program was not publicized. It was not exactly a well-kept secret, however, since the first day an executive walked up to a supervisor and startled her with the comment, "Hi! You're about to be PEETed." The team leaders learned to live with the ambiguity and make the most of the conversations.

Not all the executives were faithful practitioners of PEET, but those who were reaped unexpected rewards. There was a one-for-one correlation between areas that were excelling in the quality process and bosses who incorporated MBWA/-PEET in their way of doing business. One of the vice-presidents admitted meeting people who had been with the company for over ten years but that he could not honestly remember seeing before.

One executive with good intentions, but a poor track record over the first few months, found a way to ensure his own compliance with what he admitted was a good idea. In fact, he had been one of the originators of the program. He gave his PEET sheet to his secretary and had her call to make appointments for him. Then he had to go. He embellished the idea by having his secretary schedule a full hour for a visit, and he made the personal commitment to spend any time that he did not spend with the specific PEETee wandering around talking to other folks.

The reaction of some of the PEETees was classic as they tried to deal with the idea of the president of the company, a very well-liked but shy man, stopping by to chat. The effort he made to say thanks was doubly appreciated, at least most of the time. One supervisor up to her ankles (and beyond) in paperwork offered a departure. The president walked up to her desk and asked her if she had a minute to talk. "Not really," came the harassed response. "I'll call you," was his reply. Unfortunately, the supervisor had no idea that it was a PEET visit, and an anxious moment or two passed before things were resolved. The subsequent visit was a success.

This was not an isolated incident. At the end of one twenty-minute conversation, a supervisor told a vice-president, "You know, it's really nice of you guys to do this, to come talk with us. I really appreciate it. Thank you." The vice-president was unsure who had PEETed whom.

To further help top management assimilate the changes the company was making, another Zenger-Miller product, "Toward Excellence" had been introduced in early 1984. This was a video tape and workbook course put together by Zenger-Miller and Tom Peters, and it addressed the main points introduced in *In Search of Excellence*. The format was such that it prompted discussions, evaluations, and specific plans for action.

Selling "Toward Excellence" to The Paul Revere was the easiest sale the Zenger-Miller representative ever made. The fact that its philosophy coincided with that of the Quality Has Value process was no accident. *In Search of Excellence* had been a source of inspiration and ideas when the Quality Has Value process was defined.

In addition to being a vehicle for periodic day-long sessions for the president and his staff, "Toward Excellence" was added to the company training schedule for the next level of management. By both pointing out real examples of excellence and providing a format for discussion, the workbook helped to ensure that concrete steps were planned to start an audience on the road to improvement.

The Field force required a different approach to translate theory into action. Chapter 8 makes reference to some of the inherent difficulties. The introduction of Quality Has Value was considered of paramount importance, and several alternatives were suggested. If money were not a consideration, the best system would be to transport all 1,250 employees in the Field force to one location for a one-week course on quality in general and the Quality Has Value process in particular. Barring that, the next best plan would be to bring the heads of the 115 offices together, the method used the following year by AVCO Financial Service of Canada (described in Chapter 9). At the time of the discussions in early 1984, however, there was not yet any evidence that the Quality Has Value process would save or generate enough money to justify an immediate expenditure of this size. After all, established theory warned against expecting any results from small action teams for the first several months.

The Paul Revere devised a third option—to call the eight regional vice-presidents to the Home Office for a three-day meeting, to instruct them, and to send them back to spread the word, one office at a time. In preparation for the instruction of the vice-presidents, and to give them some aid in their subsequent presentations to their Field offices, a video tape was produced by the Director—Quality Team Central.

Video tapes presented one huge advantage when the problem was the dissemination of information, through several intermediaries, to over 100 separate groups. They ensured that at least part of the message was presented to every audience in precisely the same way. A second advantage came from the flexibility of the form itself. A video tape made it possible for the Home Office to write, film, and edit precisely the message it wanted to send.

The tape consisted of three parts. After a short opening statement and invitation to join in the process by the company president, three vice-presidents whose names were familiar to the Field force (including the Operations Vice-President) were interviewed in talk-show format about quality and The Paul Revere. The tape concluded with a ten-minute interview with Hall of Fame basketball player Willis Reed. Long known as a quality athlete, Reed explained what the term meant to him and how a continual striving for quality had been a major focus of his life.

After seeing the video tape, the regional vice-presidents were instructed both in the concept of quality and the general approach to achieving quality, using, in part, the same group Action material that all the Home Office team leaders had received. They were then called upon to help design the mechanics of the outlying unit version of the Quality Has Value process. Some differences in procedures for the Field force were obviously necessary.

It was decided that quality ideas from Field offices would fall into two categories. If the change had been implemented in the office itself, then the idea could be certified by the regional vice-president, with a copy of the idea and its certification sent along to Quality Team Central for score-keeping purposes and to trigger recognition as due. Some ideas, however, would require certification by Quality Team Central.

When cooperation and/or implementation by various departments in the Home Office was necessary, the quality analysts would become champions for the idea. The ideas were first presented to Quality Team Central, who became advocates in presenting them to the appropriate people and departments, and certification was granted to implemented ideas.

While the recognition program would parallel that of the Home Office (with numbers proportionally reduced the first year to reflect the exact date each office officially began the process), there would be no assessing of financial worth of ideas implemented by the Field force. The chances for consistency in calculations were too low to even make an attempt. Recognition would be based solely on number of ideas certified, either by the regional vice-president or by Quality Team Central. During 1984, the first year of the process, Field teams reaching silver or gold could choose their awards from the same gift catalogs used in the Home Office. In 1985, while Home Office employees received Paul Revere gift certificates, Field employees received gift certificates from the high-quality mail order store, L. L. Bean.

In addition to the video tape, the regional vice-presidents were also loaded down with other pamphlets and materials to help in their presentations. One, designed to be left behind with the office head after the quality introduction meeting, was titled "OK, I've Got A Quality Team...Now What Do I Do?" The opening paragraphs were:

> The team leader in the Home Office had an admitted advantage over those in the Field. For one thing, each team leader went through a series of classes to prepare him/her for conducting efficient half-hour Quality meetings. Additionally, the team leaders could easily check with each other on what worked and what didn't.
>
> The Quality Team leader in the Field has some unique advantages, too. Being in a more entrepreneurial, competitive environment should increase both the desire to improve Quality and the ability to do so.
>
> Once your team members believe that their ideas will be considered and, if appropriate, acted upon, your problem will probably become keeping track of all the ideas and prioritizing implementation.

In fact, you will most likely be surprised by the variety and number of ideas. Even in the very best of offices there are many things done simply because "that's the way we've always done it." Many employees never put forward good ideas simply because nobody ever offered to listen or set up the mechanics to make it easy—and danger free—to speak up.

The first step is to schedule your meetings. Don't just schedule one meeting, schedule at least three months in advance. By doing so you will be "signalling" your people that this is for real—and that you intend to stay at it.

The discussion of differences between Home Office and Field teams turned out to be quite accurate. Their isolation from other teams made it easy to delay doing the many little things that are necessary to establish a habit of quality. Even so, 557 ideas had been submitted, with 140 of those certified by regional vice-presidents and 76 implemented and certified in the Home Office by the end of 1984. In 1985, the first seven months saw another 1,337 ideas, with 355 certified in the Field and 206 certified by Quality Team Central. This equates to approximately 111 ideas per 100 Field employees. While this seems small in comparison to the number of ideas per employee at the Home Office, it is still a very respectable number. The National Association of Suggestion Systems reported in 1984 that in the 900 organizations it counts as members, the average number of suggestions per 100 employees was seventeen for a twelve-month period.

The Home Office added two additional classes during the first year of the Quality Has Value process. One was as a direct result of a quality idea; one reflected the change in corporate culture.

During a PEET visit, one supervisor mentioned that she wished that new employees learned more about the quality process when they first joined the company, so they could begin contributing before they got caught up in doing things just because "that's the way we have always done it." The supervisor's point was a good one. New employees are normally hesitant to say, "This sure seems to be a strange way to do things" during their first days or weeks on the job. Because of their fresh perspective, however, they were in a position to be very valuable to a Quality Team, especially if no one could explain why things were done that "strange way."

New employees did receive a brochure outlining the Quality Has Value process (see Figure 6-2), but it was one of many pieces of paper that they received. As a result of the supervisor's observation, a half-day class on quality and the Quality Has Value process was added to the new employee orientation. Telling new employees that the company welcomes their fresh ideas on how to improve operations was occasionally met by doubting looks. Offering new employees power over their jobs is not, after all, a standard approach. Once the neophytes understood that the procedures for making change were available to any employee, just waiting to be used, the approach was enthusiastically accepted.

A decision to formalize the goal of participative management resulted in additional classes for management. Like the decision to begin the entire Quality Has Value process, it was a business decision. In the Quality Has Value process, the goal was quality; in participative management, the goal was to have managers seek the input of their subordinates whenever possible; in both, a stronger company with higher profits was expected.

Experience with the Quality Has Value process supported this development. All Quality Teams and Value Analysis results came, in some degree, from the interaction between management and nonmanagement employees. The managers were already looking to their subordinates, at every level, for solutions or, at least, input. In this case, the beginning of participative management predated the theory.

Early visions of Quality Has Value had anticipated that the most active teams would be from management since they were familiar with problem-solving techniques. When the rules for qualifying for most valuable team honors were defined, any team consisting primarily of second vice-presidents or above was barred from winning. "After all," one senior vice-president joked, "saving $50,000 is easy... it's just a matter of which one of us goes first." The rule proved to be superfluous; no team consisting of upper-echelon management was even a contender for honors at year-end. The active Quality Teams were almost exclusively composed of

The Quality Process

Upon joining The Paul Revere you will find yourself soon being assigned to a Quality Team and you will hear many things about "Quality." It's all because of Paul Revere's Quality Has Value Process.

The first thing to understand is that it is a *process*, not a program. This is not something that will be completed next month or at the end of the fiscal year. It is an integral part of The Paul Revere way of doing things. It is part of our culture.

The most important feature of The Quality Has Value process is that the managers and supervisors at every level look to their subordinates for ideas. Information, recommendations and ideas flow both ways.

This, of course, means added responsibility for everyone. If a Paul Revere employee sees a way to improve The Quality of his or her job — or to improve the way their departments operate, they are expected to say so. And to be ready to help implement the improvement.

The Quality Team

The structure established to enable this process to unfold is anchored on The Quality Team. A Quality Team normally has about 10 members and, where possible, they work together in the same department or unit. The Team Leader has received special training in conducting meetings and helping a group solve problems. Quality teams usually meet for a half hour every week.

A Quality Team's primary aim is to improve the Quality—both in fact and in the eyes of the customer—of the things the members work on from day to day. The Quality meeting may only be a half hour, but concern about Quality is a continuous activity.

If a Quality Team determines that a particular improvement will not only increase the Quality of the work they do but will also impact other work areas, it is up to them to coordinate with the other people. Coordination is kept as simple as possible. Helping in this coordination is one of the responsibilities of Quality Team Central. (More about them later.)

If, however, a Quality Team has an idea which, if implemented, would involve a significant portion of the company, then there is another approach. Virtually all team leaders are also members of another Quality Team at a higher level of supervision or management. This "chain" can be used to move ideas up to the level capable of implementing them.

The Challenge to You

Being a member of a Quality Team will be an exciting and challenging part of your new position here at The Paul Revere. We know of no other company of our size that looks to every employee in the organization to be constantly on the lookout for ways to improve its Quality. We believe that the procedures we have established make it possible for everyone to contribute as much as they are capable of. And just as all employees contribute to the idea bank...all employees will share in the benefits as we become the very best company in our business.

Quality Team Central

To help the process along, there is an organization called the Quality Team Central. They are responsible for answering questions and offering help to Quality Teams. They also keep track of progress by teams so that they can be recognized and thanked as appropriate. As the name Quality Team Central implies, this group provides the centralized coordination for all aspects of our ongoing Quality process.

Welcome to The Paul Revere and to the Quality Process.

Figure 6-2. Quality Has Value Brochure

---

employees from lower rungs of the corporate ladder. This in part reflected the fact that their jobs tended to include more repetitive tasks, which are prone to incremental improvements, and in part because their enthusiasm ran higher. Having something to say about how to do their jobs—something management took for granted—was new to these employees. After a few tentative efforts to make sure the quality process was for real, they grabbed the opportunity.

Midway through 1984, it became obvious that the Quality Steering Committee had made a glaringly inaccurate estimate late in 1983. The bronze-silver-gold scheme was supposed to suffice for the whole year. Some teams, it was reasoned, might make it to gold by October or so, but that should be the earliest. The first team to have its fiftieth idea certified did so in April; four teams earned gold honors that month, with all four using the fifty ideas route rather than $50,000 saved. All were nonmanagement teams.

It was natural to give some structure to this evolving reality by formally calling on all managers to make a deliberate effort to be more participative in their management style and more supportive of their subordinates. Classes explained the theory of participative management to those in managerial positions. The division heads followed, conducting small meetings with their people to discuss the concept and ask for ideas on how to put the theory into practice. Participative management did not happen overnight. However, having the policy stated, the public commitment, and the acknowledgement in internal documents that a manager's "adherence to participative management practices" would join "support/involvement in the Quality Has Value process" as job evaluation criteria combined with existing conditions to make a definite change in corporate culture.

Publications

The first issue of the monthly newsletter, *Quality News*, was distributed on March 1, 1984. The lead articles were titled "Why Quality?" and "First to Bronze," and reflected the newsletter's dual purpose—celebration and explanation. The former began:

> Why the big emphasis on "Quality" all of a sudden? Weren't we doing anything right before?
> Those questions have been asked, or mumbled, by Paul Revere employees as the Quality Has Value process has been put into place.
> First of all: yes, we have been doing many things quite well.

The fact that The Paul Revere is a strong company in a competitive field proves that.

But we can be better. If we can improve our Quality in Fact *and* in perception our company can achieve prominence and will grow—something that will benefit all of us.

What makes our Quality Has Value process not only unique but well-fitted to our goals is that the solutions are being sought from within. We didn't turn to outside consultants to define yet another system to be tried for a limited period of time.

The Quality Has Value process was defined by Paul Revere employees. Some help has been brought in to assist with specific pieces for a limited time, but for the most part, our "consultants" are the people who have the best view not only of the problems but of the points that, while not problems, can be improved. Our consultants are our people.

The seven bronze teams which were celebrated included five that had made it on ten ideas and two that had amassed savings over $10,000. Quotes from the team leaders were included:

When they [team members] see that someone is paying attention to them, they can't wait to have another Quality meeting to attack the next problem...I can't get them to shut up.

They all love being able to say what they want to say, and that makes a big difference.

On the front side of the March 1 issue of *Quality News* was a bulletin regarding the first team to make silver status. Goldfingers, a Quality Team composed of the key punch section, had completed their twenty-fifth idea just before the end of February.

—UPDATE—
Goldfingers team has reached the Silver level—
members are picking their prizes

See Figure 5-2 for a sample of a later issue of *Quality News*.

To help keep the message consistent and to explain "nuts and bolts" items to the team leaders, another piece of communications was established. Dubbed "Notes and Ideas," it was published on the fifteenth of every month and served to

> ## Why "Quality"?
>
> Why the big emphasis on "quality" all of a sudden? Weren't we doing pretty well as it was?
> The answer to the second question is "yes, but . . ."
> The decision to launch a major effort to improve the quality of the products, services, and information provided by The Paul Revere is a decision to strive to fulfill our potential.
> Our goal is defined as meeting our specifications; Quality in Perception is meeting the specifications of our customer.
> A "customer" is anyone to whom we provide products, services, or information. That can mean the policyholder or the Home Office, or an agent, or a secretary in a brokerage office. If each of us treats the next person in line as a valued customer, the result will be Quality.
> That's why the big emphasis — to encourage all of us to think about our many customers, and to make meeting their specifications, and our specifications, our goal. Quality in Fact and **Quality in Perception** . . . **The Paul Revere.**

Figure 6-3. Quality Field News—1st Issue

broadcast ideas with general application, to give hints on how to handle particular problems, and to provide information about the process.

To encourage, and perhaps stimulate, Quality Team activity in the Field, two publications were born. One was *Quality Field News*, a one-sided cousin of *Quality News*. Its first issue was published on July 10, 1984, with the lead article titled, of course, "Why Quality?" (see Figure 6-3). *Quality Field News* was published on the tenth of each month. The other publication was initiated several months later as a means of sharing ideas. "Field Force Quality Ideas" consisted of a list of recently certified ideas that were chosen because of the possibility of their being adopted by other teams or offices. It also carried notice of impending systemwide changes. Like "Notes and Ideas" it dealt with the nitty-gritty details of the Quality Has Value process.

Posters and bulletin boards were also used to reinforce, celebrate, and inform. A "Quality Is Good News" bulletin board was established first in one area, then in several, all at the instigation of team leaders. The originator stated that "When one of our customers.... writes to thank someone for a job well done, we'll post it so that everyone can see that a quality job is being recognized."

Publications primarily constitute one-way communications from the company to the employee. While "Notes and Ideas" and "Field Force Quality Ideas" were based on information gathered from employees, the growth of the Quality Has Value process required utilizing additional means for receiving information.

Feedback

On his way into work one morning, the Director—Quality Team Central was engaged in conversation by one of the supervisors who had been in a groupAction class he had taught. She was now a team leader, and the process was about one month old.

> Team leader: "I'm having a lot of fun with this quality thing. It makes you look at your job a whole different way."
> Director: "That's great to hear."
> Team leader: "When people have a complaint now, you can tell them to look at it, to see if it can be done another way."
> Director: "And maybe you can change it..."
> Team leader: "Makes people think they're listened to... makes them feel worthwhile."

The conversation was never reported in *Quality News*, but it was typical of comments the members of Quality Team Central were hearing throughout the company. The aggregate of these conversations was a powerful indication that the Quality Has Value process was on the right course. Equally positive were stories that began to circulate about particular teams; new company heroes were emerging and were talked about with respect and affection.

One of the early pockets of excellence was the cafeteria. The ideas were abundant, but one thing held the two teams back. Neither of the women who were the Quality Team leaders in the cafeteria had ever used a computer before. In fact, one had never even typed. They knew, however, that if their teams were to be recognized for their efforts, they would have to use the Quality Team Tracking Program. Instructions in hand, the two trooped off to the nearest terminal. The story was that the programmer sitting at the next terminal had to be helped away from his terminal, weak with laughter, before the two determined women got their data entered; but both teams made it to gold, and both team leaders—including the nontypist—signed up for a self-taught programming course.

Feedback is not always positive, but it always deserves attention. Awards were presented in informal ceremonies as described in Chapter 5. The importance of having one of the Co-chairman of the Quality Steering Committee conduct the presentations of bronze and silver awards (the company president presented the gold awards) was driven home the first time a substitute was used. Even though the replacement was necessary (both co-chairmen were out of town) and the replacement was also a division head (a member of the president's staff), the quality analysts were asked the next day why the teams had not "rated the first string." It was early 1985 before a replacement was used again—and then with some trepidation. This time, there was no complaint; the process was secure and the recipients of the award seemed almost to welcome a new face.

By paying attention to the first negative reaction, and delaying its repetition, unpleasantness was avoided. A valuable lesson was learned: until a process is established, every permutation, no matter what the intent, will be noticed, and the worst possible interpretation will at least be considered.

Conversations and stories are only two types of unstructured feedback, actions also provide insight into changes taking place. As more and more teams became comfortable with the idea of quality, ideas and suggested guidelines began to be unofficially traded throughout the company. One team leader proposed this description of "good service":

1. It is fast.
2. It does not require the customer to restate his request (or complaint) to several people before the correct one.
3. It is courteous.
4. It does not subject the customer to any requirements or inconvenience because of "company policy."

5. It does not require the customer to furnish information the company already has.
6. In short, it does not inconvenience the customer for the sake of the company.

This list was not published or endorsed by management, but it circulated nonetheless, which says a great deal about the pride that this team took in having come to terms with this issue. It also says a great deal about the change in corporate culture that other teams did not see this as encroaching, but instead used the list for their own purposes.

In all of the cases cited here, the information gained was a by-product. These were not attempts to check the progress of the Quality Has Value process or to gather data as a basis for subsequent decisions, although both types of results occurred by inference. To supplement such happenstances, information was actively, even aggressively, sought.

Quality Teams had never really had the means of knowing how well they were doing in the eyes of their many customers. People had worked on their Quality in Fact, albeit perhaps not with that specific phrase in mind, but what impact their efforts were having on Quality in Perception was, for the most part, unknown. Attempts were made to change this situation. The informal approach consisted of hundreds of conversations, ranging from simple "How am I doing?" to long, detailed discussions reviewing a variety of characteristics about the interface between two units. One of the primary results of these information exchanges was the discovery of superfluous actions.

An attempt that fell between the formal and informal was put in place by the Human Resources Department. Cards labled "How'd We Do?" were printed and placed in convenient spots. The flip side of the card asked for any "comments, complaints, suggestions, or compliments." The person filling out the card had the option of requesting a direct answer. The cards went to a committee consisting of one member from each of the three Quality Teams in Human Resources.

Surveys, a formal means of "listening down"—and in every other direction—also became a normal routine. A survey should never be conducted unless the person or unit asking the question is prepared to share the results, good or bad, and is committed to doing something to correct any low spots. Once an employee group believes that their survey responses will be taken seriously, they will be more precise in their answers. It is a cycle that can only benefit an organization. Surveys used included those put together by the market research section of the company and one industry attitude survey.

The market research department built three separate surveys: one polling the Home Office employees, one for the Field employees, and one for the "ultimate consumer," the policyholders. In all three cases, the questions were very specific, asking for opinions about such points as courtesy, accuracy, and promptness of particular departments. The information was turned over to the division and department heads to be used as a source of ideas and as a benchmark against which to compare the next year's survey.

The results of the industry survey were used as a basis for immediate action. The attitude survey showed that overall the employees thought fairly highly of The Paul Revere. There were areas in which the percentage of positive responses was low, either relatively (to the industry average) or absolutely. The latter was considered a point of concern, even if the industry average was low.

The method chosen for reacting to the results was the formation of action teams. The areas of concern were divided into six groupings: supervision, job duties and training; chance for advancement and job security; work group climate and communications; work schedules; physical setting; and salary and benefits. A call for volunteers was issued. The action team members were chosen from those who came forward, taking care to include a mix of pay grades and departments.

The team was then assigned a resource person, someone with expertise in the area of concern and the ability to track down answers to any and all questions the team might develop. The team was told to work out their own schedule but that it was estimated that they should have a set of recommendations within a couple of months. After presentation of their recommendations to the company president, the team would be disbanded.

Each team's list of recommendations was distributed to every employee as an assurance that the team's work would not result in just another report filed deep in someone's drawer. By making the recommendations public, the company management put pressure on itself to react quickly. A cover letter signed by the president accompanying the first list read in part: "I have received the first report on supervision, job duties and training, a copy of which is attached. I think the report is a Quality job and should be implemented. The implementation plan has been incorporated with the report."

The Quality Has Value process both spurred innovation and crossed departmental lines. The entire company—in Quality Teams—discovered that it could try new projects on its own. When a Quality Team found itself unable to fully pursue an idea, it could go to Quality Team Central, who advertised themselves as "champions for hire." The quality analysts helped implement workable ideas, including those ideas that involved several departments, with all credit going to the initiating team.

Value Analysis

At the end of each Value Analysis workshop, participants returned to day-to-day activities with a list of recommendations. As the year progressed, it became apparent that implementation of these recommendations happened less quickly—and in a less uniform fashion—than originally projected. Implementation was not actively resisted; lack of time was the culprit. The problem, of course, is that once the workshop ends, the participants have to go back to oiling squeaky wheels and plugging leaky dams.

Unlike Quality Team ideas, which receive immediate reinforcement through formal recognition, Value Analysis ideas tend to become part of the job without fanfare. Recompense for completion is more abstract: peer recognition, satisfaction over having improved the output of the department, and personal recognition of the immediate supervisor.

The most effective means to stimulate implementation proved to be the Director—Value Analysis and his assistant. By their interest, reminders, and offers of assistance, they helped to refocus attention on the essential purpose of the work unit. "Refocus" is the operative word. This is not direct pressure, which tends to result in emergency fixes with long-term weaknesses.

Some teams continued adding recommendations to their list long after their workshop was completed; all teams found that the essential purpose proved invaluable as a touchstone for decision making, whether in setting new policy or changing old. Like the Quality Teams, the Value Analysis Workshops stressed a creative approach to routine tasks. "Why am I doing this? Is there a better way?" could be answered more surely with the essential purpose in mind.

The positive results of Value Analysis were unmistakable. For many management groups, the Value Analysis Workshops were the first time the "team" had ever sat down and specifically talked about philosophies of management and professional goals. The increased knowledge about each other gave a long-range cohesion to the teams that provided a context—as well as a vocabulary—for solving problems. The improved communication between participants and their greater appreciation for one another proved to be one of the major benefits of the workshops.

7

Quality Has Value: The Second Year

The first year of Quality Has Value (QHV) astonished everyone. After logging over 7,100 ideas on the Quality Team Tracking Program in 1984, the worst case scenario envisioned QHV '85 with a mediocre start, trailing interest, and a natural demise. This was based on "common wisdom" about such efforts: employee involvement/enthusiasm would peak within the first year of its existence and begin to lag thereafter. Optimists hoped that making a few changes in QHV '85 would keep it viable by focusing on areas where progress was possible. Maybe results would even match 1984. The optimists were wrong; Quality Has Value accelerated as its entered its second year, and 1985 surpassed 1984 in every respect.

Determining the Cost of Quality

Advance planning for Quality Has Value 1985 included a Cost of Quality census. A Cost of Quality estimate made in 1983, before the launching of Quality Teams or Value Analysis, provided information on the company before the QHV process; a census taken in February 1984 furnished detailed information to use as a basis for comparison in later years. The 1984 census was an adaptation of a procedure recommended by

Phil Crosby in *Quality Is Free*. Where Crosby defined three categories (prevention costs, appraisal costs, and failure costs), the Quality Steering Committee used these four:

Prevention: training in new procedures, systems testing
Detection: reviews of work balance, control
Correction: redoing work that included errors, computer reruns
Failure: "correction activities resulting from errors, not being on time, or nonconformance which requires corrective action, rework, and/or special explanation, *but in addition*, the particular item has been received by the final customer"

Every team was directed to list the amount of time each member devoted to each category in an average week plus any specific costs incurred by variations from quality standards. The numbers were not precise, but rather were best estimates. The final number gave an indication of the magnitude of the problem at hand, served as a source of ideas for the team throughout the year (when in search of an idea, a team could always turn to its Cost of Quality census), and acted as a benchmark by which to measure the team in years to come.

In this census, the employees estimated that of the time devoted to quality, 45 percent was spent on prevention, 25 percent on detection, 18 percent on correction, and 12 percent on failure. An overall figure of 44 percent of work time spent on quality was "amazingly consistent among divisions," according to the vice-president and assistant treasurer responsible for tallying the figures. The consistency tended to confirm the theory that a whole series of good faith best estimates would add up to a valid number, as the high estimates and the low estimates balanced each other.

In early 1985, Quality Teams were called on again to spell out how much of their time was spent on quality efforts. This time, however, the objective of the census was given as the cost of nonconformance. It was more than a whimsical semantic change. It was instead a recognition that it is not quality that costs; it is nonconformance, or nonquality, that is expensive.

Quite simply, it costs less to do something right the first time than it does to have to correct it later. If the item has already reached the final customer, the error not only costs immediate dollars, it also jeopardizes future sales. Both Quality in Fact and Quality in Perception are affected. David Garvin quotes Richard W. Anderson, general manager of Hewlett-Packard's computer systems division, as saying:

> The earlier you detect and prevent a defect, the more you can save. If you throw away a defective 2-cent resistor before you use it, you lose 2 cents. If you don't find it until it has been soldered into a computer component, it may cost you $10 to repair the part. If you don't catch the component until it is in the computer user's hands, the repair will cost hundreds of dollars. Indeed, if a $5,000 computer has to be repaired in the Field, the expense may exceed the manufacturing cost.

Another computer giant, IBM, estimates that 30 percent of its products' manufacturing cost—the total Cost of Quality, prevention, detection, and appraisal—arises directly from not doing it right the first time.

While the realistic possibility of zero defects may be debatable, its value as a goal cannot be. Those who packed parachutes in World War II had no problems with the concept of zero defects *after* they were told that they would, on a random basis, be required to make jumps occasionally with the parachutes they had prepared. Employees often assume zero defects without realizing it; they object loudly if their paycheck is wrong, yet even an accuracy rate of 96 percent results in two incorrect weekly checks each year.

The 1983 Cost of Quality estimate had been taken at the direction of the parent company, AVCO Corporation. Two men made a very rough guess and set the Cost of Quality figure at $9,659,000. In 1984, by converting time into wages and adding material costs, Quality Teams determined that the Cost of Quality was closer to $16.2 million. The 1985 figures were calculated in the same manner as the year before. In 1985, not only did the final tally decrease from $16.2 million to $14 million—a per capita decrease of 14 percent—the percentage of total time given to quality decreased from 44 percent to 41 percent, and the time devoted to each category of quality effort shifted significantly. The results of the 1985 cost of nonconformance survey gave strong evidence that Quality Teams and value workshops had been effective, that the company had begun down the right path in its efforts to become a truly quality organization.

The 1985 census showed 41 percent of work time devoted to quality. The shift in emphasis in 1985 was reflected in a 5 percent increase in prevention and a 5 percent reduction in time devoted to correction and failure (see Figure 7-1). The combined costs of correction and failure—the real cost of nonconformance—went down by 16.7 percent.

Achieving quality is expensive, except when compared to not achieving quality. The costs of initiating and sustaining a quality process are new and obvious. The costs of not paying attention to quality are costs to which firms have become accustomed, invisible parts of every budget. Further evidence to support the cost effectiveness of quality can be found in a study commissioned by the American Business Conference and conducted by McKinsey and Company, Inc., over a two-year period. As reported in the November 1984 *Planning Review*, 81 percent of the companies responding to the survey assessed their products to be above industry quality levels; only 51 percent of the respondents reported above-average costs. "Therefore," the authors conclude, "they produce at least 30 percent of their products at above-average quality for average or below-average costs. Several of the CEOs...claim to have both the highest quality product on the market and the lowest production costs." Quality *is* relatively free.

Providing a Focus

During the first year of the Quality Has Value process, there had been no specific focus promulgated. Teams were simply told to take steps to improve the Quality in Fact and in Perception of what they did. For the second year, it was decided that a more targeted approach would be both possible and appropriate. Many teams, after all, had directed much of their energy toward eliminating irritations and generally making their internal operations run better during the first year. They were now ready to look outward.

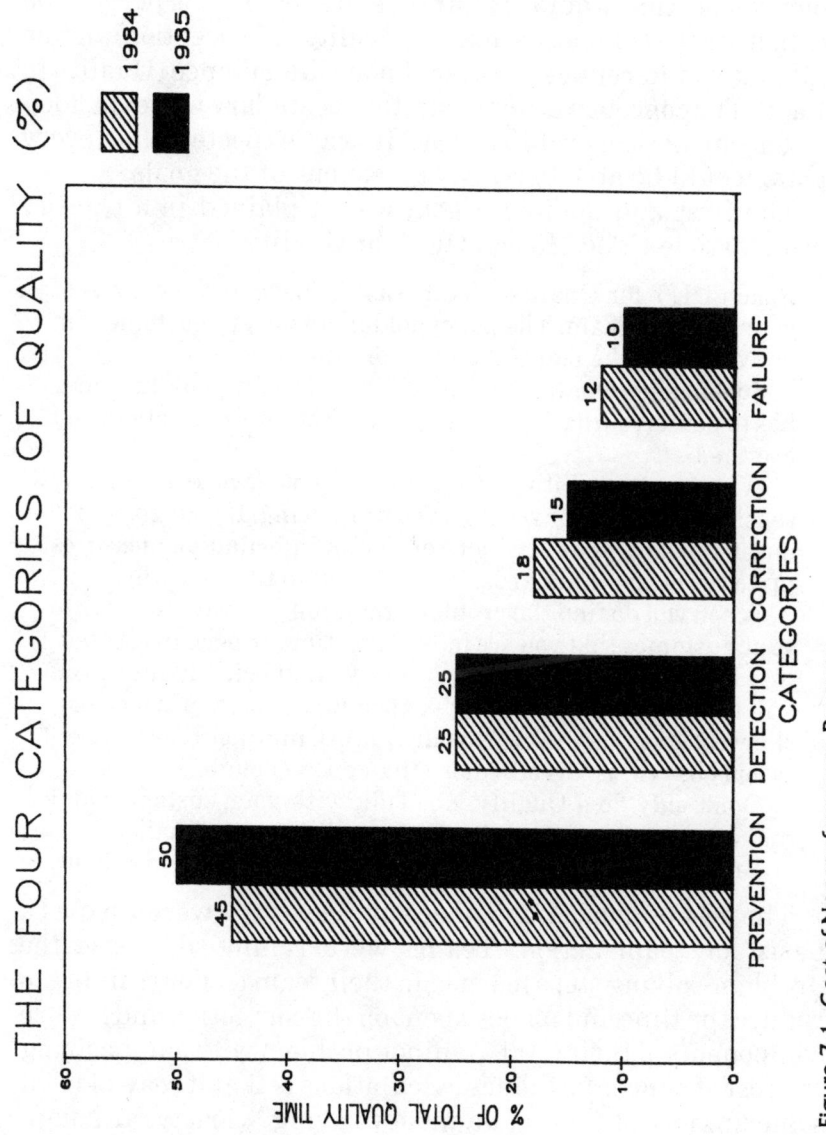

Figure 7-1. Cost of Nonconformance Progress

The tack taken was to identify the dual nature of quality with two goals. Teams were urged to concentrate their efforts on projects that would (1) improve the customer's perception of their or the company's quality (Quality in Perception) and/or (2) that would reduce the cost of nonconformance (Quality in Fact). The concept was the same; the vocabulary was expanded to encourage concrete actions. It was expected that every team would be able to reach at least one of the goals.

The first and dominant goal was explained in a *Quality News* article titled "Reach OUT for Quality."

> Reach OUT for Quality—OUT, that is, beyond the bounds of your Quality Team. The policyholder, and every customer "in between" are the rightful objects of attention.
>
> Just doing a Quality job isn't all there is to it! Your customer has to perceive what you do as Quality; they have to believe you are the best.
>
> Whose responsibility is that? **Yours.** You have to listen, to be sensitive to whatever reaction you are getting. If your customer doesn't believe your product, service, or information measures up to his or her standards, it's up to you to find out why.
>
> When you do find the problem, then you will have to prove to your customer that you are indeed meeting, or perhaps exceeding, his or her expectation; or raise your specifications so you will be meeting the customer's expectations; or, as a last resort, show the customer (a) why your Quality may not reach expectations but (b) is already more than good enough.
>
> Don't only do a Quality job. Talk with your customer and make sure you are receiving due credit for your Quality.
>
> Brag a little. There's plenty going on worth bragging about.

The cost of nonconformance survey results were used as a basis for team action. Teams were reminded to use the problem-solving steps learned in their team leader training to reduce the time and money spent on the correction and failure components of their total. A minor problem with emphasizing the cost of nonconformance calculations is that it reawakened some anxiety of the "just a money saving" variety, although there was less resistance than expected. After spending a year making money-saving estimates to present to the quality analysts, most teams were well aware of the relationship between time and money and its relationship to corporate strength and job security. This is an important point, especially if a company is attempting to initiate a quality process when the majority of the work force—union or not—is openly suspicious of them.

Other practices that served to keep Quality Teams focused on the desired goals utilized the quality analysts, the recognition system, and increased publicity. For QHV '85, quality analysts were directed to ask "Does this have an effect on your customer's perception of your or the company's quality?" and "Does this reduce your cost of nonconformance?" It was made clear to all teams that judging of teams and individuals for monthly and year-end Most Valuable Team and Most Valuable Player honors would rely heavily on meeting the dual goals for QHV '85. Other ideas were equal in that they still counted for recognition purposes, but they were definitely "less equal." The announcement of the policy concerning monthly honors for teams and individuals read: "Near the end of each month the Quality Team Central analysts will look over the ideas certified during that month, looking for teams and individuals that have done a particularly outstanding job in positively impacting their customer's perception of Quality or in reducing their Cost of Nonconformance."

At virtually every presentation of quality pins and gift certificates, the Co-chairmen of the Quality Steering Committee would ask the team members what they had done toward the two goals. Posters produced by the secretary of Quality Team Central appeared. The importance of the customer and the customer's perception and the need for reduction of the cost of nonconformance (see Figure 7-2) were alternated with other posters.

Modifying Quality Has Value—Team Leaders

Quality Has Value '85 inspired very few modifications and additions on the theory that "If it ain't broke, don't fix it." When it began, the most significant alterations were:
1. A specific focus was given for Quality Team efforts.
2. The material elements of the recognition program were changed (see Chapter 5).

132   Commit to Quality

The cost of nonconformance is the cost of doing it wrong.

Figure 7-2. Quality Poster

    3. Awards for MVT and MVP were modified (see Chapter 5).

    4. Awareness efforts such as posters and short-term programs were added.

    5. Teams were encouraged to change team leaders.

Quality Has Value: The Second Year 133

The last provision proved to be a real strength of the 1985 process. At the suggestion of the company president (newly returned from an AVCO quality tour of Japanese factories and companies), the invitation to switch team leaders had been issued at the end of 1984. Up to that point, most team leaders continued to be the organizational superior (at whatever level) who had been there since the beginning. Not everybody is a natural team leader; some do not do a particularly good job even after training. In some cases when the organizational head was also the Quality Team leader, his or her position was more inhibiting, if not intimidating, than helpful. In keeping with the move toward participative management, the role of Quality Team leader was a good place for a nonmanager to learn or hone some leadership skills. Leading is made easier and learned more quickly when the followers are eager to reach the same goals, as is the case with the Quality Has Value process.

It had also been noticed that natural job shifting within the company acted as a boost to QHV '85. As people left active Quality Teams and joined units that had been slow to get going, they served as catalysts for moving a Quality Team out of the starting blocks. It was theorized that having new team leaders might also result in renewed activity. New team leaders were immediately enrolled in the groupAction course that had proved itself so valuable in preparing people both to conduct meetings and direct problem-solving sessions. Additional offerings of the course were added to the training schedule early in the year to handle the turnover. By mid-1985, less than half of the team leaders were from the original group.

Zealous response to the new goals set for QHV '85 was due at least in part to this large-scale change in team leaders. The reorganization also contributed to the emergence of new pockets of excellence within the company; new team leaders brought some areas of the company alive that had barely reached bronze, or possibly silver, the year before. In other areas, completing Value Analysis set the stage for departments to finally get active in the Quality Team aspect of Quality Has Value. Happily, these newly active teams were joining the 1984 exceptional teams/areas, rather than replacing them.

Some former team leaders became members of the team they once led; others simply dropped from the team, while continuing as members of their superior's team. The interlocking nature of the original Quality Teams was weakened by this development, but habits of communication were well enough established to survive. Management and nonmanagement were a great deal more comfortable with one another at the end of QHV '84, but not without working at the change.

It was as if neighbors had decided to replace a six-foot wall with a four-foot fence. With a wall, there was no question whose property was whose. It was easy (even if not very satisfying) for one side not to think about how the work was done, knowing that a few mistakes were "only human" and would probably be overlooked, and that any improvements were somebody else's responsibility. On the other side of the wall, responsibility and authority was less complex (if not as effective) when workers did not raise any exceptions to decisions. A quality organization cannot survive a wall. A fence, however, is a different matter. A fence does not merge the property, but it is low enough so folks can comfortably lean on it and talk across it, and a few lock-free gates add an atmosphere of friendliness and trust.

Beginning Again

The 1984 Quality Celebration generated enthusiasm which helped QHV '85 get off to a good start. As much as it marked the end of the first year of Quality Has Value, the Quality celebration served as a positive beginning of the second year. Many people who had hesitated before fully "buying in" came across the line after this demonstration of the numbers of employees actively involved in the process. The Great Hall of Mechanics Hall, where the celebration was held, has a large main floor and a horseshoe-shaped balcony. Winners of awards were from gold teams, and a request was made for silver and bronze teams to sit in the balcony so that winners could reach the stage more easily. When the company president asked everyone who was on a gold team to stand, virtually all of those seated on the main floor, close to 750 people, rose. It sent a powerful message; nothing could have been clearer than that the Quality Has Value process had the support of the majority of employees.

Going into 1985, management assurances that the Quality Has Value process was a very real part of doing business and was here to stay were believable. It was also apparent to the most casual observer that most employees accepted the system as a means for both personal and company growth. When one team leader was asked when she thought the number of ideas would begin to slow, she answered, "Why should it? The employees are used to changing things themselves now, and as long as the world around us keeps growing and changing, the ideas will keep coming." Her assessment held true through 1985. What was already one of the outstanding employee-involvement processes in America accelerated as it entered its second year.

The tremendous start to 1985 owed much to the foresight of The Paul Revere employees (see Figure 7-3). It had been announced in advance that on December 1, all team counters would be reset to zero, that is, all Quality Teams would start the new fiscal year even, with no ideas and zero savings toward recognition. Seeing this coming, some teams stepped up their efforts in October and November in order to get to the next level of achievement before they lost credit for what they had on the books. Others stopped reporting activity on the Quality Team Tracking Program.

One of the ten double gold teams for 1984, for example, was not sure if they would be able to complete fifty more ideas before December 1. So they left all their ideas on the Quality Team Tracking Program with a status of "1," while working through their list. On November 22, a quality analyst was invited to their area for the morning. He arrived to find three team members and a small mountain of "proof" paperwork waiting for him. Three and a half hours later, the team was triple gold.

Another double gold team was not able to complete the next fifty so they waited until December 2 and logged thirty-five implemented ideas onto the system. They were a gold team before Christmas.

136 *Commit to Quality*

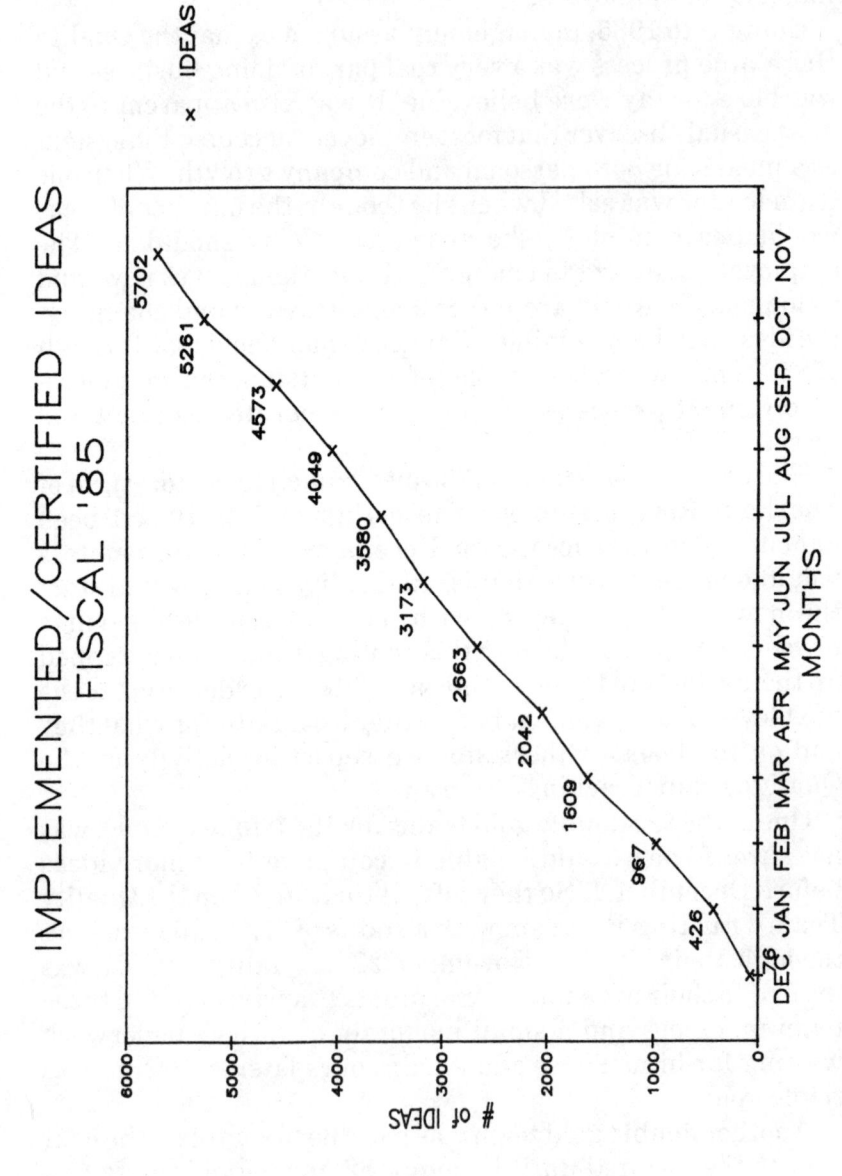

Figure 7-3. Quality Has Value 1985—Certified Ideas

By February 1, 1985, there were already four gold teams, eight silver teams, and twenty-one bronze teams. A month later, thirty-four more bronze teams, twelve more silver, and four more gold teams were added to the rolls. Several milestones were reached by the end of June 1985. Notice the comparison dates in 1984:

100th bronze team—August 1984

6,000th idea—logged on in early September 1984

3,000th certified idea—September 1984

$3 million in annualized savings—late November 1984

These figures are even more dramatic when contrasted with a look at the 1983 suggestion system results prior to QHV '84. In 1983, 216 suggestions were submitted. The 86 accepted suggestions totaled $41,000 in savings. These figures were in line with the national averages computed by The National Association of Suggestion Systems.

Also by February 1, Value Analysis had completed twenty-eight value workshops, generating more than $5.5 million in estimated annual savings. Value Analysis workshops were quick to take advantage of the "We can—and should—change things" attitude engendered by the Quality Team concept.

The momentum carried into 1985 continued throughout the year. A comparison of QHV '84 and QHV '85 appears in Figure 7-4.

	1984	*1985*
Ideas Logged on the QTTP	7,135	9,250
Ideas Certified	4,115	5,702
Annualized Savings	$3,250,000	$7,459,531
Bronze Teams	127 of 128	123 of 125
Silver Teams	101	117
Gold Teams	72	104
Double Gold Teams	10	48
Triple Gold Teams	1	12
Quadruple Gold Teams	0	4
Quintuple Gold Teams	0	4
Sextuple Gold Teams	0	1
Septuple Gold Teams	0	1

Figure 7-4. Quality Team Results—The First Two Years

138 *Commit to Quality*

The Paul Revere Companies WORCESTER, MASSACHUSETTS 01608-1528 • TEL (617) 799-4441
Our policy is quality.

AUBREY K. REID, JR.
President

November 21, 1985

To All Paul Revere Associates

What gives the Paul Revere the strength and vigor to survive in such a competitive industry?

I've thought about that question often during 1985.

One answer stands out among many...quality. The difference between quality and non-quality is broad. Quality enables a company to capture loyal customers with products that do the job they were designed to do. Quality enables us to nurture customers with service that understands and cares. Our people enable us to deliver on our quality promise.

Paul Revere people, in the home office and in the field, have committed themselves to quality, and have dedicated themselves to meeting our corporate goal of becoming the leader in the North American insurance marketplace. That kind of commitment and dedication is what gives the Paul Revere its strength and vigor.

As Thanksgiving time nears, I extend my sincere thanks for your exceptional efforts.

Best wishes for an enjoyable Thanksgiving and a Happy Holiday Season.

Sincerely,

Aubrey K. Reid Jr.

The Paul Revere Companies
The Paul Revere Life Insurance Company • The Paul Revere Protective Life Insurance Company • The Paul Revere Variable Annuity Insurance Company
Affiliates of AVCO CORPORATION

Figure 7-5. Thanksgiving Letter from the President

The Paul Revere recognizes that once the employees are let in on the decision making, the company can turn back only at great peril. Employees will give back their recently granted authority, but very grudgingly. An aborted quality process does not just return a company to its starting point; it is a singular failure with far-reaching consequences.

Here there was no question of failure. President Aubrey Reid's Thanksgiving Day message 1985 reflects The Paul Revere's commitment to quality (see Figure 7-5). The Paul Revere is not a perfect company with uniformly participative managers and enthusiastic employees who wake up in the morning thinking quality thoughts (although at least one team leader did report waking up in the middle of the night and writing down an idea for possible implementation by her team). But in just two years, it is a stronger company, a better place to work, because quality is a part of the "way we do things around here."

8

Listening Down— And Out

The Quality Has Value process lends itself to a blend of three types of leadership: authoritarian, participative, and delegative. The term "listening down" best describes the essence of this crucial blending, and it is deceptively simple in concept: pay attention to the people who work for you.

Listening down is built into the American psyche. One of the strengths of the American form of government as defined by the Constitution is that it institutionalized listening down. The members of the House of Representatives are on the shortest leash, with only two years between elections, and they tend to have the most active mechanisms for listening to the people. Everyone in government is subject, ultimately, to recall if they choose not to listen.

The president and others often urge that people write their elected representatives, trusting that the exhortations on a particular point will become so insistent that only those seeking early retirement will choose to be deaf. The withdrawal by the United States from Southeast Asia can be debated on many levels, but there can be no doubt that it was spurred by politicians influenced by public opinion. (Mr. Gallup and Mr. Harris have amassed tidy fortunes by providing stylized means of listening down.) Governments with no requirement to listen down (e.g., the Soviet Union) are not as efficient or as attractive to potential immigrants.

As with governments, so it is with business. Given a choice, people will choose to live and/or work where they have reason to believe their thoughts will receive some consideration, where they will be listened to. The country or business that fosters such an atmosphere will be more prosperous, even if they do not achieve perfection.

Recognizing a Pattern

American managers will agree, at least in principle, that listening down is desirable; most will even claim that they do it. In practice, however, "listening up" is all too often the common mode of communication in American industry. All their corporate lives, managers have been told, implicitly and explicitly, that wisdom comes from further up the corporate ladder. One listens up and gives orders down.

The assumptions that create this mindset are strikingly similar to the authoritarian management style. The authoritarian style consists, unsurprisingly, of telling subordinates what should be done and how it should be done, without seeking any input in advance from the subordinates. For example, when John Wayne addressed his uniformed subordinates with "All right, listen up, you guys," on the silver screen, there was no doubt what he meant. They were about to get "the word" from their superior, who had both information and authority that they did not have.

Variations of this theme include: (1) only those at the top of the management ladder understand the complete problem, and (2) most managers have worked their way up to their current positions, thus giving them a credible understanding of what they are asking from their subordinates. Everyone regards a slow rise in the company as the natural state of affairs. One of the least respected figures in American folklore is the boss's son (or daughter, as the years wore on) who held his or her authority without earning it, regardless of the talent of the individual. The only condition more despicable was to marry the boss's offspring. In reality, the manager who began a career "on the loading docks" and rose to be the company president has always been a rare individual.

Even in the cases in which the manager has worked his or her way up through the ranks, assuming that you remember other employees' attitudes is a dangerous delusion. The executive feeling that "I've been there (in the sales force, or the mail room, or whatever); I know what things are like there" is precursor to the feeling that talking to the people currently employed in those jobs is not necessary. Unless his or her rise to the top has been truly meteoric (i.e., it took less than three months), things have changed since the manager worked there.

Many managers also behave as if they are bringing their expertise to bear to avoid a crisis—no matter how routine the matter. When time is truly a critical factor, as in John Wayne's case in which bullets whizzing past emphasized the need for immediate action, the manager may be the deciding factor in warding off disaster. But this is not always the case. In the day-to-day management of business, there are equally important considerations that make listening down a more appropriate management style. A noncrisis approach may, however, be less ego enhancing.

The function of management is not open to debate. Someone does have to make tough decisions that affect the entire company; someone does have to monitor the operation of the company to see that plans progress satisfactorily. Superior knowledge and authority are here to stay, but it should be recognized that management is not inherently in possession of superior knowledge about every aspect of a task. Indeed, authority does not require mastering details of a company's operations.

Listening up as the sole communications mode for a company runs counter to common sense and experience. It is as if the communications flows through a long pipe that has a series of one-way valves, preventing any backwash, just above each input pipe. No wonder it gets lonely at the top. Corporate information does manage to dribble back up the pipe line (usually in the form of written reports, carefully massaged and sanitized by each level as it passes through), but two-way valves would be far more effective.

Companies have recognized the general inadequacy of a narrow listen up approach. For years, suggestion systems have invited, sometimes pled with, employees to get involved in improving their company. Yet, the overwhelming majority of employees pass up the opportunity. The National Association of Suggestion Systems (NASS) reported that in 1984, in those companies that reported on their suggestion system results, the annual number of ideas submitted per 100 eligible employees was 17. At The Paul Revere, in the first year of the Quality Has Value process, the average number of suggestions/ideas submitted per 100 employees was 568. (In fact, the NASS turned down a membership application from The Paul Revere. The primary reason was that the Quality Has Value process did not fit the defined criteria that suggestions be signed by an individual and submitted in writing. Additionally, an official of NASS indicated that the statistics provided by The Paul Revere would skew their average results. The NASS was, however, interested in the Quality Has Value process. A paper describing the process, submitted in response to their call for papers for their annual convention, was awarded first place).

Not all managers are insensitive louts who subscribe exclusively to the authoritarian model and act as little dictators. Many care deeply about their people, try to make the work experience a satisfying one, and listen to their ideas and problems. The move toward participative management is another attempt to enlist the efforts of employees. It relies heavily on the same precept that governs sports teams: the superiority of teamwork. A wealth of examples attest to its validity. Year after year, in virtually every sport at virtually every level, teams that appear to be sure bets because of the individual talents of the members of the team lose to groups of athletes who function as teams. The coaches of these winning teams see their players as separate people and create a format, a style, a game plan, that allows each to contribute. Not only does this enable individuals to feel good about themselves, it also brings success.

The analogy to the world of business is a useful one. Just as a coach does not listen to his players just because the coach wants them to be happy, a manager should not listen to his juniors just because doing so will make them feel good. Making it possible for each employee to take pride in his or her work and the company is of practical worth to the company. A wise manager listens because employees know things that he or she does not, such as what is really going wrong or creative ways to improve something that is not necessarily broken as yet.

Some employees do not wait for permission to solve problems. They just fix things and do not tell anyone about it—often with deleterious results. The "Fred retired" syndrome is such an example. Company A contracted with company B to produce a cast-iron piece that company A had been making for itself for many years. Company B was provided with the plans and the mold and proceeded to produce the part. For five years there were no problems; in fact, company A accepted 100 percent of the parts. Suddenly acceptance dropped to zero. Company B was sure that nothing had changed; company A was equally sure that they could not use any of the parts because of a large burr on the surface. An investigation—rather frantic on the part of company B—turned up the fact that Fred of company A had recently retired. Fred was the man at company A who had worked with the part before company B started to make it; and he was the man who first handled the part after it arrived from company B. He knew about the burr. Company A had produced the part with the burr. Convinced, however, that no one would welcome his observation that there was a burr, he simply removed the burr before passing the piece along.

There are "Freds" inside of every company, people who know unique things about how to make the system work despite itself. They are not willfully withholding information; they just don't think anyone will listen to them. A quality process is designed to change that perception, but someone must truly listen.

Overcoming Management Resistance

Once the decision is made to work toward becoming a quality company, a firm most likely will face few problems getting top management "on board." In part, this comes from their having been the ones to make the decision in the first place. It is always easier to support a decision you helped make—one of the underlying tenets of the whole quality process. Top managers' relative willingness to listen down is also symptomatic of why they are top managers, why they have risen out of the middle management pack. They habitually listen down—and sideways—and up. What brought them success has been in part their acceptance of the idea that others are capable of thought. They may even have stolen an idea or two along the way without credit to the originator. Top managers are not directly threatened by the input of ideas from the low end of the totem pole. The ideas keep the middle managers hopping and help profits. Top management jobs are in no immediate danger from a diffusion of authority.

The biggest resistance to listening down will come from middle managers who, if they consciously admit it to themselves or not, are destined never to rise above middle management ranks. These middle managers are busy expending a great deal of energy consolidating their current position rather than seeking new heights and responsibilities. They are like mountain climbers who have reached a point in the climb when they know deep inside that they do not have the talent or the nerve to make it to the next level, but they also do not want to go back down and begin a climb up a different mountain. So they become experts on how to get to their level and at how to make the way station as comfortable as possible. These same managers do not welcome implications that they do not know everything about the region beneath them. It implies that they are not fully in charge.

Since the responsibility to nurture a quality process through its early months lies squarely with management, including middle managers, this attitude is particularly troublesome. At any point in the quality process, but especially at the beginning, the rule of "once burnt, twice shy" holds. Every employee who is patronized, or simply rebuffed, will be that much more difficult to win over and so will all that person's friends. Unfortunately, it is like the "Attaboy/Oh, damn" rule. Doing something right earns you one "Attaboy!" Doing something wrong gets you one "Oh, damn!" Sadly, one "Oh, damn" wipes out up to a hundred "Attaboys." An "Oh, damn" takes on a life of its own traveling the corporate rumor route. While conscious efforts, including using company publications, should be made to spread the good examples, these efforts will be futile against the grapevine if middle management consistently provides "Oh, damns."

It requires thorough preparation, persistence, and payoffs to overcome knee-jerk negativism, the attitude of, "Well, I tried it once and nobody would tell me anything—so let's spend our energies doing real work." Preparation begins with an understanding of what listening down is and is not.

It is not an unequivocal denial that authoritarian management can be appropriate. Note that in the sports world there is never any question about who is in charge. The coach does not surrender the responsibility or the authority that go along with being the coach. Anarchy and chaos are not what is being advocated here, but the coach must recognize that the members of the team are individuals worth listening to both as players and as people. The blend of authoritarian and participative management styles is necessary.

Listening down is also delegative. The provision in the Quality Team structure for implementing ideas and *then* having them certified assures incorporation of this management style. In many cases, a manager can treat subordinate units as "black boxes." At each level, the manager defines desired output in hard product, service, or information as appropriate. The unit is provided with the support necessary to accomplish the task. The internal workings of the unit are not a day-to-day concern of the manager.

Listening down is not laissez faire. The manager needs to stay abreast, in general terms, of the evolving changes and improvements within the black boxes because he or she is accountable for the output; but day-to-day changes are of little or no concern. If trouble develops, then it is time for action—action that begins by asking the subordinates what they think is wrong and how it should be fixed. In most cases, the folks nearest the problem have some idea of how to remedy it, or at least the information necessary for the solution. Striking the balance between listening and giving input is essential.

Since the responsibility for the successful operation of the black box still ultimately rests with the manager, the authoritarian management style is also available as a tool. The judicious mixture of all three types of management is the key.

Establishing Mutual Trust

Listening down takes trust. Managers must trust employees enough to ask for help; employees must feel secure enough to respond. An employee is not automatically smarter than the boss. But each person knows something—maybe a little thing—that the boss has never even considered, and the sum total of all the knowledge and experience of a group of workers is an invaluable resource just waiting to be "exploited" by the right boss. It will not be given to just any person who expresses a desire for it or tries to force it out, but like Excalibur, it will come out with apparent ease for the right person.

What if, however, a manager has a sneaking hunch that he or she is not the right person? Further preparation is necessary in this case. Listening down takes courage. It takes self-confidence to say, "I want to hear your ideas on how to improve our operation," and to mean it. This is particularly true if a suborganization, a division within a company, for instance, has decided to launch its own quality drive. It takes guts to say, even if only implicitly, "Unlike the other managers at my level, I don't know it all. I need your knowledge. And I promise to listen." This self-confidence is an attribute of leadership more than of management. Only the self-confident can lead; the insecure can only manage.

It may be reassuring to acknowledge that listening down also involves two-way responsibility. Those employees being listened to should, after all, say something worth listening to; but judgment of the value of ideas is subjective. Many changes suggested will be minor. In fact, they will seem inconsequential, which should be a clue as to how out of touch the manager is with the individual worker. These workers have suffered minor irritants on their job. They know that they are minor but they are unwilling to make the effort to gain approval for change from the person one or more levels higher who has the authority to remove the problem. "Little" things hamper productivity, detract from the ability to do quality work, and depress morale. Given the authority to make improvements, including minor ones, the corporate world suddenly becomes a friendlier place. Remove a series of irritants that have been bugging people for years, and they are free to start thinking about bigger and more objectively important matters.

One obstacle to the worthiness of employee ideas may well be the completeness and timeliness of the information the employees are receiving. As with computers, the axiom "garbage in, garbage out" applies. If the company executives hold all information close to their vests, they should not be surprised if the employee ideas are disappointing. What Stanley Peterfreund, president of Stanley Peterfreund Associates, Inc., calls "constituency management," or the involvement of all members of the work force in the decision formulation and execution functions, is only possible if the employees are well informed and the climate for communications in the work place permits, indeed encourages, open exchanges of views, information, and ideas. Two-way communications in listening down requires the sharing of information and power, which is a disincentive for managers unsure of their ability to hold onto their job. If all the ideas of a Quality Team seem to be missing the point, the manager must look carefully at how much of the problem is with the team and how much is a problem of information being withheld from it.

Not that every employee suggestion will be a sound one. Most unworkable solutions will be stopped by peers in the Quality Team meetings, but some will surface. Managers can again make a difference. Out-of-hand rejection can severely cripple the process. As with the "Oh, damn" syndrome, many will hear that the idea was ignored; few will hear what the idea was. Explanation of a "no" is essential, and the ensuing discussion often provides a source of new insights and ideas for both the manager and the person who made the suggestion. The goal is to keep suggestions coming. The next idea might be the multimillion dollar one.

Just as the manager may feel unwilling to trust employees to produce worthwhile ideas, the employees may not trust the manager enough to lay themselves open for the disappointment that would come if their ideas are rejected. Depending on a particular manager's (or the previous manager's) track record, his or her subordinates may be quite reluctant to trust the person, especially when a quality process is young. Employees may have to be courted. The courting is the managers' responsibility. Dr. Deming has been quoted as saying,

> There will be no room for managers who do not know how to work with their people to produce high quality goods at low costs. High reliability cannot be secured without worker cooperation.... In the competitive worlds of the future, companies which have not mastered these ideas will simply disappear. There will be no excuses.

While not everyone will be willing to take the risk involved in putting their idea(s) forward at first, it is a bet—a good bet that gets better—that more people will buy in as time passes. The phased buy-in will occur naturally, and it is itself a blessing. No process could handle the flood of ideas if everyone decided on the first day to contribute all the thoughts they have been storing up over the years about how to improve the Quality in Fact and Quality in Perception of their unit or the company as a whole. The experience at The Paul Revere has been that most of the time the information and ideas being offered are well worth listening to; and, the longer the process is sustained, the better the information and ideas become.

Employees may also be suspicious of the underlying motives of a sudden shift in management techniques. No employee is likely to misinterpret the fundamental reality that a corporation moves to a quality process to increase corporate profit. He or she may be confused about the way in which the company intends to do it. This is a reflection of the confusion on the part of management. The message must be clear: this is not an attempt to get employees to work harder, it is an effort to get them to work smarter. An American Productivity Center report states, "Though it has become something of a cliche, managers have been slow to grasp the fact that people do not have to work harder, just smarter. And they have been reluctant to provide the leadership necessary for working smarter." "Overmanaged and underled," is the way Don Alstadt, chief executive officer of the Lord Corporation, has described American industry.

Listening down will move a company toward what Lawrence Miller, author of *Behavioral Management: The New Science of Managing People at Work* calls for when he says,

> It is time to replace this divisive class system with a competency continuum that recognizes the reality that every employee must participate in management and perform productive work, from the factory worker to the chief executive officer. It is my experience that workers possibly more than any other group within our corporations, are prepared to accept new relationships and responsibilities. They no longer want to be separated from responsibility. They want to participate in the business game, and they want to play to win.

Nurturing New Habits

Mutual responsibility, mutual trust, and two-way communication will avoid most of the negatives, but preparation is only half of the solution. The second half is persistence. A good start, a poor start, any start at all must be backed by a structure that provides for the nourishment and growth of the process. A quality process may even be thought of as a big mechanism for enabling ideas to flow up—the aim of listening down. By providing a format, a set of rules that you can check yourself against, it is possible to win the involvement of many who would draw back from a free form, more natural procedure. Form can precede content. The objection was raised at The Paul Revere—and will be at other places—that making something like listening down into a mechanical process cheapens it, robs it of its spontaneity. Yet, once the decision is made that this relationship will work—and that it will work to the mutual benefit of both parties—a lasting relationship becomes possible. It requires a willingness to work at it until it becomes natural. Many are the stories of prearranged marriages that, over time, became true love stories.

As with the other pieces of the total process described in this book, there are mechanics suggested as starting places.

The Quality Teams outlined in Chapter 4 are such a mechanical device. A program for establishing a habit of Management By Wandering Around (a wonderful way to listen down, named at Hewlett-Packard and popularized in *In Search of Excellence*) is described in Chapter 8. It is referred to as PEET, the Program for Ensuring that Everybody's Thanked. To break old habits, new habits must be substituted.

A central spokesperson, a champion, is essential to persistence. Somebody has to consider the quality process the most important business of the company. Even if the effort is limited to a division or a section, quality must still be given priority in order to succeed. In terms of time, it can be a part-time effort; in terms of commitment, it must be full-time enthusiasm and zeal. This individual must be seen as more than a visionary; he or she must have real power to change things. If the champion is the head of a division, the problem is nonexistent, but a company spokesperson for quality must have the backing of top management. The spokesperson cannot be a voice crying in the wilderness.

Informal listening down is an excellent way to convey commitment. An example of informal listening down described by the *Wall Street Journal* is provided by Richard G. Rogers, President of Syntex Corporation (a pharmaceutical manufacturer), who eats "breakfast each morning at 7:30 in the employee cafeteria in Palo Alto, California. Over coffee and toast, he queries employees, and in exchange he is often asked to give career counseling and advice." The *Wall Street Journal* goes on to say, "management based on direct knowledge offers benefits that outweigh being aloof and out of touch."

The head of a unit that is intent on changing and improving cannot simply announce that listening down will now occur (perhaps as a first step toward integration of participative management) and then disappear back between the in and out baskets. And, again, there is some risk. Managers who are accessible should not always expect to hear good things. At Tandem, where Jim Treybig (pronounced, what else, try-big) has made listening down a natural part of their corporate culture, a new vice-president found that out. The story was reported in *Industry Week*. A new company policy was sent via electronic mail to all Tandem employees. Within 24 hours the vice-president received over 400 messages—all of them critical. Treybig summarized the vice-president's reaction, "He said he believed in our 'people philosophy,' but it would take awhile to adjust to this democracy."

Formal or informal, the example of top management cannot be overrated. If the senior executives are actively and obviously listening down, then middle managers will do it, even if their initial motivation is mimicry or survival. When instituting a policy of listening down, a company must remember the power of symbols. Most groups of employees have lived through one or several hot new programs that were given up when there turned out to be no real commitment from top management, or the novelty wore off, or a particular champion left. Active listening down is a powerful sign that this time the change is for keeps.

Listening down should not be restricted to work matters. While not really an integral piece of a quality process, having complete counseling capabilities helps convey the message that the company does care. Counseling services might include career counseling, current job counseling, and personal problem counseling. The last includes, but is not necessarily limited to, drug and/or alcohol abuse information. The counselors can be either company employees or from an outside agency or some creative combination of both. The payoff is a more loyal employee who will, although perhaps unconsciously, redouble his or her efforts to contribute to the company. And, of course, since problems sap energy, their solution frees a person to concentrate on the job.

The easiest way to formalize listening down is to borrow a chapter from Gallup and Harris and do a survey. Surveys provide a means of large-scale listening down for an organization intent on learning the attitudes and level of satisfaction of either its external customers or its work force. Satisfaction is another way of saying that the organization in question is living up to its customer's expectations. A survey as a check of Quality in Perception can be used both as an immediate source of ideas and as a measurement of trends. It can be homegrown or a product of professional associations querying industry standards. The advantage of the former is that the questions can be specifically targeted, while the latter provides comparison against results received by similar companies.

Surveys raise expectations. At least they do until the potential respondents feel that "Nobody's done anything as a result of the last several, so why bother?" Therefore, a company should be sure to have a follow-up plan in mind before conducting any survey. To increase response, the follow-up plan should be announced along with the survey. This is particularly imperative with an organization's own work force, but the promise of action need not be limited to work force surveys. An attempt to build a loyal customer base could include a pledge to listen to the customers, followed by changes, followed by a second mailing describing the changes "because you wanted us to make them."

A decision to proceed with a survey and to promise to reveal the results and take action on them means that the questions must be carefully worded to yield specific answers. Simply to ask, "Are you happy here?" is useless since nothing will be learned about the cause of any unhappiness (and some is sure to be surface) or what could be done to change it.

A survey used in the context of a quality process can be an invaluable resource for the individual departments within a company. By constructing the surveys to ask the employees their opinion of the quality of the departments' performance (broken into specific categories), the results can serve as both general motivation ("I didn't know we were thought of that way!") and inspiration on specific ideas ("According to this, an awful lot of people think our response time is lousy."). A follow-up survey (e.g., six months later) will demonstrate to all concerned the areas where progress has been made and where it has not.

Industrywide surveys are particularly useful for defining areas of concern that need the attention of a quality process, in part because they provide not only the reactions of the employees of a specific company, but they also contain industrywide information. In answer to a particular question, for instance, it might develop that the company's employees give the company a positive rating of 80 percent. If the industry average is 95 percent, the high scores takes on a different meaning.

As with any form of listening down, the important thing is not only to hear the words but to react to them. Time is a critical factor if changes are to be identified as resulting from the survey. Once questions about the company's policies and programs are raised, they must be addressed officially and promptly. Survey results must be made available as quickly as possible, and public pledges to work on any specific points must follow. If a survey is to have any impact on Quality in Perception, doing the right things in response to a survey is only half the equation; making sure the work force or customer knows that the changes were the result of their input some weeks or months before is the second half. The longer the lapse, the more difficult it is to make this connection.

Extending Listening Down to the Field

Those in outlying units need a special sort of listening. They require listening intense enough to overcome barriers of physical distance reinforced by the cynicism spawned by previous experience.

An adversarial relationship is, after all, almost inevitable. The thinking in the field, where "the rubber meets the road," is "if those high-toned muckety-mucks back there had any understanding of all I have to do to keep this company afloat, if they would bend just a little in my direction for a change, there wouldn't be any problems." In the central office, the thinking runs more like "if those prima donnas in the field would just read their mail and follow a few, simple, necessary rules, there wouldn't be any problems." The 9-to-5 hours of the people in the home office ("They are never there when I need them") are resented; the flexible hours and freedom of movement of the field representatives ("They are never there when I need them") are equally resented.

One thing that both work forces are likely to have in common is a negative. The field (or sales) force has also seen many short-term, high-pressure programs and contests come and go. Convincing them that the concern about quality will become a part of corporate culture will be difficult.

The physical separation makes it even more difficult to address this issue. The field units are separated not just from the central office, but also from other company entities. Quality Teams benefit greatly from being in an atmosphere conducive to their activities. It is not so much peer pressure, although that can certainly be felt by a team that is lagging behind the average, as it is peer leadership, acceptance, and encouragement. Quality is contagious, and the more people there are around to spread the contagion, the better.

Quality Teams that by circumstance must operate in isolation must be the object of active, obvious listening. What may appear at first glance, or to toughened authoritarians, to be coddling or hand holding is not only necessary, it is perfectly appropriate. Unable to sense the excitement that is a natural mood of a quality process in operation handicaps a detached Quality Team in comparison to its home office counterpart. Transmitting that feeling via announcements, newsletters, phone calls, and video tapes is difficult. One way to overcome the barrier, at least in part, is to gather all the field Quality Team leaders in one place periodically (see the AFS/Canada example in Chapter 9) and trust them to transmit not only the information but the inspiration back to their team members. If they are convinced that this quality thing is for real, they can infect their associates with their enthusiasm.

Even after such an expensive beginning, however, persistence will be required. It will be complicated, because many of the ideas generated in the field offices will require the cooperation of various people within the home office for implementation. Not many of the ideas from a central office Quality Team require the involvement of a Quality Team Central (by whatever name) to coordinate with other Quality Teams; the percentage of ideas from the field that cannot be implemented without the involvement and approval of a home office Quality Team is, however, quite high.

Four requirements are necessary if the field efforts at quality are to be successful. The first two are for each outlying

Quality Team to spend time 1) assessing its own efforts and 2) working to improve its own Quality in Fact and in Perception. Next, the outlying Quality Team must adopt the perspective of the home office as a valued customer and provide it information and service of the same quality as that provided to the paying customer. The fourth necessity is that the home office return the courtesy.

The occupants of the central office must make it obvious that they are listening down—and out. During the initial months of a quality process, many of the ideas that will come from the field will be "old" ideas, favorite projects of individuals who have been proposing them for as long as anyone can remember and who have never understood why "Those deaf SOBs don't recognize a good idea when it's right in front of them." A quick check will most likely reveal that there are valid reasons for the suggestion being turned down in the past and why it should be rejected again. But the odds are also high that the response heard by the idea's initiator has been a cursory "No." No explanation has been understood or accepted, even if tendered. Under the same conditions, a paying customer would simply have gone elsewhere.

When these retread ideas are submitted via the quality process, it is imperative that they be answered in great detail, even though they are being rejected. It may seem paradoxical at first, but ideas that must be turned down rate more attention and in-depth study than those that are accepted and implemented. Converts to quality can be won by well-documented rejections, just as well as they can be won through acceptance. The point is to make sure that the Quality Teams out there in East Overshoe know and believe they are being listened to; or like the paying customer, they will not buy again.

Maximizing Benefits

Preparation and persistence by themselves will not establish listening down as a permanent part of corporate culture. What makes new habits stick is the payoff. The payoff for the company has always been clear: increased profits. Whether or not the payoff has occurred will be equally clear. The payoff for the individuals in the company is more subtle. For the managers, the payoff is in becoming a leader, not merely a manager, and the personal rewards that come with getting things done in a relatively hassle-free environment. A fallout from that increased competence is likely to be promotion within the company, especially for those who have best mastered the skills of leadership.

For the employees, the payoff is in attaining a status of team member, rather than the status of a typewriter or other piece of office equipment. It is more difficult to tell when this has taken place, although retention rates serve as a clue. The flip side of payoff—penalty—also serves as a clue to whether listening down is taking place.

A manager who chooses to ignore the input received from juniors—particularly one in an organization that is actively soliciting input—is acting in a professionally suicidal manner. At the least, the manager will lose relative ground to those peers who are listening down and thus improving the output of their units. Depending on the personalities involved, the manager can also be set up for a major fall by his or her subordinates. When your peers and friends are excited about their ability to influence their job environment and product and you know that your boss is denying you the same opportunity, it is time not only to get mad, but to get even. Any manager at any level who does not think that subordinates can do severe damage to the manager's career is a master of self-delusion. True, the manager may be able to "take a few of them with me," but so what? The subordinates involved will feel a great deal of self-righteous satisfaction, and the lower down the scale, the easier it normally is to find a new job.

The behavior of employees on the job will also indicate whether listening down is occurring. If the ideas dry up, watch out. A work force will stop producing ideas if cued to do so. It will grow to accept its place (what choice does it have?) and settle in to do the minimum required to draw a paycheck. And why not? In many ways, it is easier. After all, if you have no influence on the way things are done, how much grief can you possibly get when things go wrong? And even if, unfairly, you do get some heat, you at least know where justice lies.

Such a manager's subordinates will sit back and survive, or they will become ex-employees. It may appear that these employees are a small loss, since their perceived productivity is probably very low. Training a replacement appears to be worth the cost of getting rid of dead wood. In all likelihood, however, the same employee, given a chance to solve problems, could become productive without additional expense. The cost of not listening down is often hidden.

It is not just the bottom rung of employees who leave because no one is listening. Middle managers who are on their way up (or at least still believe themselves to be in the ascending phase of their career) have the hope of being able to "fix things" once they rise to the appropriate level. All have lists, many of them actually written and ready. When Admiral Elmo Zumwalt became the Chief of Naval Operations for the U.S. Navy in 1970, the story circulated that he walked into his new office on the first day on the job with a notebook containing a list titled "Things I will do when I'm the boss"—a list he had been building for years. He proceeded to change the Navy profoundly.

What if Zumwalt had not become the Chief of Naval Operations? The odds were heavily against it, simply because of the numbers involved and because he might have left the Navy at any point. Young managers face long odds, and they get discouraged. Given the professional mobility of many young executives, they might not stick around until they reach sufficient seniority to fix whatever it is. Why should the company lose those ideas or have to wait five or ten years for an idea that may then be outdated? Why not tap this source while the ideas are current and the originators are still with the firm?

All hyperbole aside, listening down is hard work. It does pay off for everyone, at every level. Profits increase, jobs are more secure, and the workplace is a more hospitable environment. There is no choice but to give it a try. The alternative is abysmal.

9

Adopting Theory and Adapting Practice

The success of the Quality Has Value process at The Paul Revere is not unique or lucky. The principles behind it can be and have been adapted to other companies, both manufacturing and service.

One example is the spread of the quality principle to The Paul Revere's parent company, AVCO. In 1983, AVCO corporate headquarters named a vice-president for quality. This executive began his tenure by making a visit to each AVCO subsidiary and stressing the importance of the quality of life, which he defined as dependent on "enjoying what you do and feeling it is important." Without it, he maintained, it was difficult, if not impossible, to achieve quality in morale or production.

In conjunction with his activities, the corporation began holding Quality Quorums—meetings of representatives from all the subsidiaries, scheduled every four months. These meetings not only sought out theories and applicable work from outside the corporation, but also ensured a useful exchange of information among the various components. At first, there was a good bit of skepticism. AVCO units include manufacturers of tank engines, consumer loan companies, the only producer of boron in the free world, and, of course, an insurance company. Representatives of these subsidiaries were doubtful that a successful quality process in an insurance company had any relevance or applicability to, for example, a manufacturer of airplane wings. But they soon learned that the similarities were greater than the differences.

Jeff Pym of The Paul Revere's Canadian head office verbalized what was a common experience. He defined the three stages of a quality process to be: "What can you do for me?" "What can I do for me?," and "What can I do for you?"

Outside the AVCO corporation, other companies have made similar efforts to improve quality, and they are enjoying success. Despite a wide diversity in the kinds of organizations, there is a striking similarity in their basic methodologies. Through all of these programs run principles and procedures that parallel those of the Quality Has Value process.

ZEBCO, Inc. is currently the world's largest manufacturer of spin cast fishing tackle, although it began its corporate life as the Zero Hour Bomb Company, a producer of electric time bombs for oil-well shooting. It operates from two plants in Tulsa, Oklahoma—one union and one nonunion.

As described in an American Productivity Center Case Study, changing markets and changing customers led ZEBCO to institute a quality process in 1982. Rather than being satisfied with the knowledge that they were producing items that had Quality in Fact, "They now direct all efforts to build a quality product, based on *customer needs*, for the lowest cost, that can be sold at a reasonable price." The emphasis on quality was spurred partially by the inroads that Japanese-made equipment was beginning to make on the fishing reel market and partially by pressure from within from employees.

In record time, the ZEBCO management put together a plan that blended employee awareness, management involvement, team action, vendor compliance, and recognition. It was, in retrospect, possible to install and sustain because, as the ZEBCO president, John Charvat, put it, "The quality of courage was always present—courage to try something different, courage to deal with all of the predictable emotions surrounding change and to keep moving forward in spite of all this." Interestingly, the "programs leading to improved quality and productivity were initiated in both plants and were managed in the same manner. Results indicate that workers have responded equally positively in both the union and non-union environment."

One program that has paid long-term dividends was the decision to have the vice-president of manufacturing meet twice each week with six different employees to discuss in detail the business indicators by which ZEBCO's success was to be measured. It took fifteen months to see all employees, at which time a second round of talks was announced. The focus of the new round was "an exchange of questions and answers" rather than "one specifically designed to improve employee awareness of the business reasons behind improved quality and productivity."

The team approach chosen was quality circles, with membership rotated every six months and management consciously shifting authority to the circles. Their efforts were credited with $33,000 in savings in 1982 alone. In addition, the circles contributed to reducing the percentage of the cost of each product that was attributed to the "Cost of Quality (Field rejects, warranty returns, internal defects, rework and scrap ratio)"; it went from 11 percent prior to the quality process to 3 percent as 1984 began.

To upgrade the quality of the material received from its vendors, ZEBCO initiated a program called "Getting Hooked on ZEBCO," soliciting suggestions from vendors for "improvements to their own components or to ZEBCO's products that could result in a reduction in the Cost of Quality or retail price of the product." Vendor-submitted proposals resulted in a total annualized savings potential of $141,000 in 1983.

The company also made inspections more stringent. There was an escape clause, however. If a component was not defective on 98 percent of its shipments over a six-month period, the vendor was certified and inspections became less frequent.

Recognition and reward, with an emphasis on immediacy and consistency, are considered an integral part of the ZEBCO program. Both individuals and groups are singled out for their contributions to improvements in quality and productivity.

The system is aimed both at saying thank you for what has been done and at eliciting further involvement through submission of suggestions or intensification of effort.

Mel Kant, the industrial relations manager, a member of the original planning group, recalls now that, "The value of involving the worker didn't come on us initially. It was a slow-moving realization, but once we could see the logic of it, we moved quickly to take advantage of every bit of help workers were ready to give ZEBCO." One of the employees, Elsie Washington, offered the view that, "Unless we do our part to make the company successful, we can't be successful as individuals."

Another quality effort is taking place at the Crown Zellerbach paper mill in Camas, Washington. It features another obvious attempt to bridge the gap between top management and the employees and to reinforce the employees' feelings of commitment to the company. Also the subject of an American Productivity Center report, the transformation of the plant into a quality-conscious, participatively managed company has been spearheaded by plant manager John Shank, who introduces himself simply as an "employee of Camas mill" and who "has met with every employee in the [2,000-employee] plant, spending a week in meetings with workers to explain financial concepts, the state of business, and the threat of competition from abroad. He regularly holds brown bag lunches with small groups of employees."

Their suggestion system is informal, with the key appearing to be that "workers at the mill had always wanted to do more than they were allowed." Cross-training and familiarity visits between departments have helped build understanding of the complete production cycle and each person's role in it. Tangible awards for improvement come in the form of gainsharing, with employees receiving annual bonuses based on production above standard. To allay fears that productivity improvements would mean a reduction in the work force, the promise was made up front that any reductions that might occur would be handled via attrition, rather than layoffs. Good ideas would not cost suggesters their jobs or the loss of a friend's job.

National Semiconductor calls its process "Quest"—an acronym for "quality enhancement strategy." It is classified by the American Productivity Center as a management system, designed to improve productivity and quality by "changing National's management style and philosophy to encourage participation and better provide employees with the tools that will allow them to achieve a more productive and positive work place." Within a few years, the company plans to have 100 percent of its 40,000-person work force operating within the Quest system.

The basic concepts that give Quest its foundation are "business awareness, mission clarification, output identification, measurement, target selection, target analysis, objective setting, feedback and recognition for accomplishment." Quest has been introduced in numerous locations in Asia, Europe, and the United States. The director of staffing and personnel, Tim Thorsteinson, reports that, "The system works well in all cultures because it is based on some very basic concepts. For example, recognition for accomplishment is important to everyone. The specific application or kind of recognition may vary from culture to culture, but the need is a constant. I believe that all successful programs have that kind of sound, global basis."

A key point in the National Semiconductor management philosophy is "Participative problem solving and decision making.... Employees are the experts in improving work methods. Whenever possible they should participate in making decisions that affect their jobs."

Results? The American Productivity Case Study reported that, "In the April 30, 1984, issue of *Fortune* magazine, National Semiconductor was awarded top honors in productivity improvement in the electronics and appliance industry. Citing a reduction in defective chips from 8,000 per million to 150 per million, the article noted that the company has also boosted sales per employee 94 percent in this decade, as compared to an industry average of 28 percent."

At Corning Glass Works, a quality process was instrumental in lowering the rejection rate of catalytic converters from 2 percent to a point where the level is measured in parts per million—and not many of them. Despite these impressive numbers, the vice-president of quality, David Luther, says, "We're trying hard to quantify, measure the results we've achieved. But right now, what is important is learning more about the quality process rather than measuring efficiency." At Corning Glass, productivity is identified as "producer concern," while quality is a "customer concern" measured by "customer satisfaction."

To this point, the examples given in this chapter have been from the world of manufacturing. And, indeed, quality programs and processes did come first to manufacturing companies and only later to service industry organizations. This has been true on both sides of the Pacific.

One service company that has made a noteworthy beginning of a quality process is AVCO Financial Services of Canada. It is an effort derived directly from the Quality Has Value process at The Paul Revere. Its objective is moving AFS/Canada "from being one of the best consumer finance companies to being the best one." Quality is especially important to a company such as AFS/Canada since they are competing in a saturated market with numerous competitors. There is little in the way of new territory to claim; market share must be wrested away from someone else.

After visiting The Paul Revere twice in 1984 and reviewing the procedures that made up the process begun there, the AFS/Canada president, Will Barrett, announced that, "I was prepared to give the operators the freedom to operate if they were prepared to be accountable."

The company has a headquarters staff of 170, and 231 branch offices scattered throughout Canada employing 1,200 people. Prior to launching its quality process, it sought to determine exactly where its quality perception stood in the eyes of the customers and employees. These efforts included:

> A personal letter to 250,000 current and past customers, soliciting a service-oriented response.
>
> A questionnaire to 900 business sources asking about the company's services and programs.

A survey of all employees asking their opinions about the company and their individual careers.

To move the management staff even closer to the customers and to signal all personnel in the company about the seriousness and intensity of the effort, the rule was established that any middle-management executive visiting a branch office had to contact at least ten customers by phone or over the counter to discuss the quality of the company's products and services, to elicit suggestions, and to thank them for their business. The requirement serves as a constant reminder to the executives of the basics, of what their employees face every day, and of the impact of things that are objectively quite minor.

AFS/Canada charged a committee with designing their "quality improvement process." They defined the "two elements of quality" as Quality in Fact and Quality in Perception in this way:

> Quality in Fact, which is achieved through first time performance in the execution of our duties and responsibilities.
> It is defined as:
>
> Doing the right thing
> Doing it the right way
> Doing it right the first time
> Doing it on time
>
> Quality in Perception, which is how our customer perceives our people, products and services is achieved by:
>
> Delivering the right product
> Satisfying our customer's needs
> Meeting the customer's expectations
> Treating every customer with integrity, courtesy, and respect.

The word "customer" was defined as "anyone to whom we provide information or service." It includes: branch customers, dealer or business sources, fellow employees, head office, anyone making an inquiry from whatever area, and another branch. The discussion on 'customer' in the AFS/Canada literature concludes: "By recognizing the emphasis that AVCO places on quality, you will understand that we all share the responsibility and are dependent upon each other for success."

The structure chosen to involve all employees in the move to quality was one of nonvoluntary Quality Teams. Training team leaders was handled by the Zenger-Miller product, groupAction, and procedures for recognition, gratitude, and celebration were very much like those used at The Paul Revere.

Once all of the pieces were defined and the preparation completed, the decision was made to assemble all the branch managers from all over the country in one place at one time for the first time in the company's history. This act not only underlined the tremendous importance given the process, it also made sure that the explanations, intents, and procedures of the quality process reached the employees in the field—the majority of the company—in as pure a form as possible.

Four days, beginning on June 12, 1985, were devoted to meetings. Branch managers were given unprecedented authority and were instructed to share the authority with their employees. Will Barrett told them that, "People must have the power to make decisions and perform aggressively."

It was a trust built on knowledge of his people, their market, and the potential of the process. Based on initial results, Barrett has declared that he is "looking at a 50 percent increase in net profit in 1985 over 1984 and we will exceed our goal of a 15 percent return on equity." This from a company that prior to the initiation of emphasis on quality suffered through a period of thirty-four consecutive months during which the number of customers dropped.

The Paul Revere Insurance Companies' Quality Has Value process exported well. It is far from being the only, or even the first, systematic attempt to improve the quality of a company; but, by its relatively lean and clear philosophy and methodology, it offers a uniquely adaptable model that can be molded to fit the structure and personality of virtually any organization. And it has proven results.

The exact procedures for winning and using employee commitment will vary from company to company, depending upon the distinctive features of each organization. Some things, however, are not optional. The entire work force must not only be invited to become involved in quality, it must be granted the authority to implement needed changes. The Quality Has Value process is a revolution—a revolution based on trust. By adopting the theory and adapting the practice, any organization—service or manufacturing, nonprofit, community, or academic—can set itself on the path to quality.

Appendix: A Blueprint for Quality

What follows is a distillation of the model that incorporates the points presented and demonstrated throughout this book.

Commitment—The Unit Boss

This will most likely be assured, since the unit boss is the one who will make the decision to begin the process. If the process is brought to the fore by subordinates, they cannot be content to simply get approval to give it a try for awhile, they must make a convert of the chief executive and gain approval of the necessary funding and time. Incorporation of phrases such as "quality process" into everyday vocabulary combined with rules/reminders (such as making quality the first thing to be talked about at every meeting), will help get out the message that the boss is really serious about quality, that it is not just another program.

Commitment—The Next Level of Management

Quality cannot be a one-person show. The first levels of management beneath the process initiator must also be convinced of the worth of the process. In fact, their jobs may well be the only ones endangered by a quality process, since giving them the choice of getting all the way in or all the way out is a very real option available to the boss. Lip service will not do; active, obvious support and involvement are needed. If, for instance, a program such as PEET is established, they must be faithful practitioners.

Those in high-level and middle-management positions will have to display a combination of faith in the process, faith in their subordinates, and the courage to be leaders rather than mere managers. A process can survive without them for a limited period, but there will come a time when a choice will have to be made—quality or obstinate managers.

The Committee

The definition of the procedures that frame the structure of the quality process is better not left to one person. The process will have an impact on every division and person in the organization. It is important to have every segment of the company feel that its views and particular needs were represented during the definition of the process. Just as no segment can be given the option to disassociate itself from the process, neither can any segment be excluded from the definition phase.

The relative "clout" of the committee also counts. Not only must there be representatives from all corners of the company, including union representation if any part of the work force is unionized, they must be men and women who are placed highly enough that they can speak for their departments with authority. As a group, they must have access to the unit head. This, of course, is a relative issue. If a department seeks improvement within a company, the committee is drawn from the levels of management within the department.

Beyond the practical issues, the prestige of the steering committee (or whatever name is chosen) will help lay the foundation for the eventual success of the process. If it is common knowledge that a group with seniority has invested a great deal of time in its definition and initiation, the importance of the quality process is emphasized before it is even launched.

Definitions and Goals

The first objective of the committee must be to determine what quality means to them personally, then what it means to the organization, and, finally, how to express that understanding in clear, concise language. The committee must bring the concept of quality into sharp focus so that the concept can be used as the touchstone against which to test all subsequent decisions. This step may involve required reading to build a common vocabulary and several lengthy, and probably spirited, discussions.

Examples of sets of definitions and goals from The Paul Revere and AFS/Canada are provided in Chapters 1 and 9, but homegrown phrasing may be substituted. The IBM Boulder's PRIDE Program uses these definitions:

> *Quality:* Conformance to requirements.
> *Customer:* The next user of the output or service.
> *Competitive*: Superior in function, cost, reliability, availability and service to any other similar product or service offered in the marketplace.
> *On time*: Meeting the committed date.

IBM also provides a set of sample goals. As reported by Robert Hayes and Steven C. Wheelwright in a *Harvard Business Review* article titled "Competing through manufacturing," IBM defines success as "having the best product quality, growing as fast or faster than the market, and being profitable."

The Plan

It may be appropriate to pull in outside help to define the procedures that will form the framework of the quality process under discussion. Depending on the elements chosen, it may even be appropriate to retain such outside help for an extended period. However, this must be in addition to, not a substitute for, corporate commitment. The control of the process in fact and in perception must not be surrendered to the consultants. If a consultant wants to modify a company's chosen approach to fit the convenience of what the consultant is used to doing, another consultant should be found. The responsibility and credit for the success of the process must be retained by the company so that employees can rightfully say, "Look what we did."

Consultants leave. A quality process is intended to be a permanent part of the company's culture. The facts mitigate against relinquishing control to a temporary outsider. Consultants can be extremely valuable, but the profession is well named.

Among the points to be decided early in the steering committee's work is how to address the dual problem of doing things right and doing the right things. Making shoddy products faster is not an improvement. Separate but complementary procedures such as The Paul Revere's Quality Teams and Value Analysis workshops offer the best of both worlds by involving every employee. The work force is given the structure for doing things better; the managers have the opportunity to use their experience and overview in deciding what are the right things to do. Undoubtedly, there are other ways to tackle these questions, however.

Whatever the approach, the acronym KISS—Keep It Simple, Stupid—should be kept in mind. Building a complicated set of procedures with dozens of variables and options may satisfy the ego, but it is also an invitation to confusion and disuse. The aim is to enlist everyone in a quality effort, not to create a handful of quality priests who are the only ones who understand the procedures. A computer program that eliminates paperwork, such as The Paul Revere's Quality Team Tracking Program, is an example of a procedure that everyone can master. It should be easy to participate.

A Value Analysis effort may or may not be made a formal piece of the process, but a network of teams must be established. Everyone must be on a team. Excluding anyone from membership sends a message. The message itself may range from "The people excluded are incapable of helping" to "The people excluded are already doing everything they do as well as it can be done." The former message is likely to be the interpretation if nonmanagement employees are excluded; the latter may be the interpretation if management is "excused" from participation. Neither message is true; both are damaging. The truth is that quality is everyone's business, including everyone on a team sends that message.

There are other advantages to enlisting everyone in the effort. The company gets the benefit of people's minds, as well as their eyes and hands, at no additional cost. By making membership on teams nonvoluntary, the process will benefit from the ideas of people who would never have volunteered and will still get the ideas of those who would have.

These teams must be more than a showcase. The transfer, no doubt down the corporate ladder, of authority is a given. It is a waste of everyone's time to build in elaborate procedures for various layers of watchdog committees. The involvement of everyone, the normal budgeting constraints, and the ownership that employees at all levels feel toward their job and the company, will serve as far more effective checks than a random group of managers who are not familiar with the procedures being discussed. Establishing a complicated, time-consuming sequence of steps to win approval of ideas also ensures that small ideas will not be proposed. Yet, it is the ability to implement small ideas that does so much toward winning the involvement and the commitment of the work force.

Bruce R. Scott and George C. Lodge describe the "new premise" underlying the role of the individual in the workplace in a paper titled "U.S. Competitiveness in the World Economy: A Problem of Premises."

> Self-fulfillment and the motivation to work hard and well stem from one's place in the community, a work group, or a corporation. Well designed groups provide the individual with the sense of identity and control needed for commitment. The art of human resource management is to design and manage groups so that each member has an opportunity to make full use of his or her capabilities and imagination to make the entire organization as effective as possible.

Another part of the overall plan will have to be a set of measures/indicators. How will the organization know when it is doing "it" well? Bean counting, that is, the type of precise count-every-little-action procedures that are often prevalent when work measurement is used, is not appropriate. Counting carloads of beans and the number of healthy bean plants—or looking to overall results and the ability to sustain those results—is. A limited number of macromeasures should be chosen and tracked. Managers will have a hard time giving up their bean counts; leaders will welcome it. The number of quality ideas suggested and implemented, the percentage of teams that are obviously active, the potential savings or extra income are all possible measurements.

Service industry settings are a particular challenge when it comes to setting goals and taking measurements. As George Odiorne points out, "The productivity of white collar workers cannot be measured without the active and full cooperation of the job holder." Belief in the process and its benefits to both the individual and the company must be secure, or any measurements will be suspect.

Training

A great deal of training will be necessary, both in preparation for the process and in order to sustain it. For the initial presentation to the company (most likely to the management contingent first, and then to the work force at large), the steering committee will need an articulate, obviously dedicated spokesperson, preferably the chairperson. One point to be addressed immediately will be why the push toward quality is being initiated at all. If the answer is presented badly, the process will take a while to recover. A quality process is not a move to recover from the errors of nonmanagement employees. Most likely, they have been doing as well as they were allowed to do. A quality process is an opportunity for an entire organization, working as a team, to improve. It is a chance for greater autonomy on the job.

A second, and equally important, point to stress: a quality process enhances job security. So many productivity programs, especially those directed by consultants whose fees depend on the amount of reductions in salaries that they propose, have resulted in layoffs that workers, particularly those represented by unions, are wary of them. A quality process, with its aim of pleasing and increasing the number of satisfied customers, will have a positive impact on incoming business and, in turn, on employment figures.

Teams and team leaders will need training. To prepare team leaders for their new roles, a course that teaches them to conduct participatory meetings and to guide a group through systematic problem solving must be purchased or constructed in-house. The nature of the work will dictate the amount of training required for team members.

Statistical quality control quite likely will be part of the course, although the emphasis placed on it and the strenuousness of the instructional segment will depend upon the nature of the firm's work. Differing opinions on the importance of statistical quality control abound. Dr. Deming asserts that, "Everyone in the company must learn the rudiments of the statistical control of quality, not just to solve a problem, but as a plan to define problems and the causes thereof." Another view is suggested by Dr. Joseph M. Juran in answer to a question posed in *Quality Progress*: "Statistical quality control is a useful thing, particularly in process improvement, process control. It is one of the important tools to use, and we're getting good results. But there are many other things that are needed, and we've got to stop regarding it as a cure-all or a panacea." Tom Peters offers the observation that "Statistical quality control is important *if* the attitude of the people is right."

While middle and top management will receive the same training as the team leaders (most of them, after all, most likely will be team leaders at the outset), leadership training is also in order. The long-range success of the quality process as well as personal success require that managers make the step up from the subset "management" to the broader concept of "leadership." At issue is the difference between controlling employees and learning to motivate and inspire them. Managers must treat their employees as adults, respect them as individuals, acknowledge that they can think, and solicit and use those thoughts. In short, they must trust them.

Recognition, Gratitude, and Celebration

Recognition of effort, gratitude for accomplishment, and celebration of success must be speedy, sincere, and fun. It can vary from a handshake to a material item to publicity or other forms of public acknowledgement. However, it must happen as soon as possible, it must be reflective of the involvement and gratitude of top management, and it must be enjoyable.

A varied core program, augmented by temporary programs, is essential. Everyone must truly hear "thank you" in a way that is meaningful to them. It is both deserved, and it inspires more quality work as a by-product.

Communications

Organizations begin with communication systems and channels, both formal and informal. Passage of time, changing conditions, and growth all too often bring deterioration. One thing that a successful quality process does is open the lines of communication that have been clogged or abandoned over the years. Supplemental procedures may also be required.

There must be a means to receive and disperse information about the quality process. Newsletters and memoranda cover one aspect; programs such as PEET address another. If company management is not in the habit of talking with employees, a program such as PEET and an orchestrated push to make participative management the norm may be needed.

Chief Mechanic

The steering committee cannot be expected to oversee the day-to-day functioning of the quality process once it has been defined and launched. A chief mechanic will have to be chosen—and chosen with care. He or she will need a trained staff to track the progress of the teams. A budget that can vary with the degree of success of the process is also necessary; otherwise, it might not be possible to say thank you to the teams and individuals past a certain point. An inflexible budget penalizes success.

In the case of a small organization, it may be necessary for the head of the unit to act as chief mechanic. Since he or she will become the most obvious proponent of and spokesperson for the quality process, an ability to teach and to make convincing presentations is required. The person will have to be creative and persistent. Above all, he or she will have to be flexible. John Henry Cardinal Newman's observation that, "In a higher world it is otherwise; but here below to live is to change, and to be perfect is to have changed often," describes the perfect mindset for a chief mechanic.

The chief mechanic and his or her staff will have to be trusted to make many day-to-day decisions needed to bring the theory defined by the committee to life in a practical world. To help provide the background for these decisions, it is desirable to identify a chief mechanic as early as possible and involve him or her in the steering committee's work. The appropriate staff must also be organized and trained prior to launching the process. Because of the dynamic nature of the job, particularly in the opening months, access to top management, including the head of the company, is an absolute necessity.

References

Barnes, Jim: "ZEBCO, Inc." American Productivity Center, Case Study 37 (1984), pp. 1–7.

Barrett, W. A.: "Success Stories: AVCO Financial Services Canada LTD." *The Achiever* (groupAction supplement, Zenger-Miller, Spring 1985), pp. 1–4.

Bigbee, Carolyn J.: "Trendsetters: Secretarial Quality Circle—the New Voice in Industry." *The Secretary* (June/July 1984), pp. 18–19.

———: "Boulder Pride Program: A Commitment to Quality." Information Products Division, IBM.

Bowman, James S.: "Why Japanese Companies in the U.S. Don't Need Quality Circles." *Personnel Administrator* (October 1985), pp. 111–117.

———: "Camas, Washington Mill Reflects Crown Zellerbach's Renewed Attention to Human Resources." *The Productivity Letter* (American Productivity Center), Vol. 4, No. 12 (May 1985), pp. 1–3.

Clifford, Donald K., and Richard E. Cavanagh: "The Winning Performance of Midsized Growth Companies." *Planning Review* (November 1984), pp. 18–23, 35.

———: "Corning Glass Works Focuses on Quality Improvement." *The Productivity Letter* (American Productivity Center), Vol. 3, No. 4 (December 1983), pp. 1–3.

Crosby, Philip B.: *Quality Is Free.* New York: The New American Library, Inc; First Mentor Printing, January 1980.

Day, Terian C.: "Strategies for Setting Up a 'Commitment to Excellence' Policy—and Making It Work." *Management Review* (May 1984), pp. 16–24.

Dewar, Donald L.: Letter to Elizabeth G. Perry, Editor, Wiley & Sons (December 2, 1985).

——— : *Quality Circles: Answers to 100 Frequently Asked Questions.* Red Bluff, CA: Quality Circle Institute, 1984.

Garand, Bruce: "Annuity Department: Employee Achievement Award Program." Internal document, The Paul Revere (1982), pp. 1–2.

Garvin, David A.: "Product Quality: Profitable at Any Cost." *New York Times* (March 3, 1985), Section III, p. 3.

Halberstam, David: "Yes We Can!" *Parade Magazine* (July 8, 1984), pp. 3–7.

Harwood, Charles C.: "The View from the Top." *Quality Progress* (October 1984), pp. 26–30.

Hayes, Robert, and Steven C. Wheelwright: "Competing Through Manufacturing." *Harvard Business Review* (January–February 1985), pp. 99–108.

——— : "Honeywell Aerospace and Defense Group." American Productivity Center, Case Study 34 (1984), pp. 1–8.

——— : "Innovation Through Involvement." Internal document, The Travelers (1983), pp. 1–12.

——— : "James G. Treybig." *Industry Week* (October 15, 1984), pp. 50–51.

Juran, Joseph M.: *Juran on Quality Planning.* Wilton, CT: Juran Institute, Inc.: First Draft, April 1985.

Kivenko, Ken: "Quality & Productivity: An Inseparable Team." *Productivity* (October, 1984), p. 10.

Lawler, Edward E., III, and Susan A. Mohrman: "Quality circles after the fad." *Harvard Business Review* (January–February 1985), pp. 65–71.

Major, Michael J.: "The Quality Measure of White Collar Productivity." *Modern Office Technology* (October 1984), pp. 160–166.

——— : "Managers Quality Conference." Avco Financial Services Canada LTD. (June 12, 1985), pp. 1–16.

Maslow, Abraham H.: *Motivation and Personality.* New York: Harper & Row, 1970.

Mazique, Mignon: "The Quality Circle Transplant." *Issues & Observations* (Center for Creative Leadership, May 1981), pp. 1–3.

McNamee, Mike: "Japanese Factories in USA Blend Management Styles." *USA Today* (September 18, 1984), p. 6B.

Miller, Lawrence: *American Spirit: Visions of a New Corporate Culture.* New York: William M. Morrow & Co., Inc., 1984.

Miller, Lawrence: *Behavioral Management: The New Science of Managing People at Work.* New York: John Wiley & Sons, 1978.

Naisbitt, John: *Megatrends.* New York: Warren Books, 1982.

Naisbitt, John, and the Naisbitt Group: *The Year Ahead 1986: Ten Powerful Trends Shaping Your Future.* New York: Warren Books, 1985.

——— : "National Semiconductor." American Productivity Center, Case Study 35 (1984), pp. 1–8.

Nelson-Horchler, Joani: "Are U.S. Workers Lazy?" *Industry Week* (June 10, 1985), pp. 47–52.

——— : "New QCC Recognition Program Offers Travel, Dinners And Gifts." *Q-municator,* Vol. III, No. 1 (January 1985), p. 1.

Nolan, Robert: Letter to Patrick L. Townsend, July 8, 1985.

O'Boyle, Thomas F., and Carol Hymowitz: "Keeping in Touch: More Corporate Chiefs Seek Direct Contact with Staff, Customers." *Wall Street Journal* (February 27, 1985), p. 1.

Odiorne, George: "The George Odiorne Letter." MBO, Inc. (December 7, 1984), pp. 1–4.

Peters, Tom, and Nancy Austin: *A Passion for Excellence.* New York: Random House, 1985.

Peters, Thomas J., and Robert H. Waterman, Jr.: *In Search of Excellence.* New York: Harper & Row, 1982.

——— : *The Pursuit of Efficiency.* Beverly Hills, CA: Roundtable Films, Inc., 1983.

——— : "Q & A: A. V. Feigenbaum, J. M. Juran, Philip Crosby (Special Report)." *Quality Progress* (October 1984), pp. 32–37.

Reagan, Ronald: Letter to the NASA Symposium on Productivity and Quality (September 24, 1984).

——— : "The Revival of Productivity." *Business Week* (February 13, 1984), pp. 92–100.

——— : "Reward Systems and Productivity: A Final Report for the White House Conference on Productivity." American Productivity Center (1983), pp. 1–16.

Reynolds, Barbara: "Inquiry: An Interview with Val Olson." *USA Today* (February 14, 1984), p. 9A.

Richards, Bob: "Providing LESS to get MORE From the Quality Circle Process." Lakewood, CO: Consulting Associates International, Inc., 1983, pp. 1–10.

Scott, Bruce R., and George C. Lodge: "U.S. Competitiveness in the World Economy: A Problem of Premises." Working paper. Boston: Harvard Business School Press, 1984.

Thurston, William R.: "Quality Is Between the Customer's Ears." *Across the Board* (January 1985), pp. 29–32.

Townsend, Robert: *Further Up the Organization.* New York: Knopf, 1984.

Tribus, Myron: "Deming's Way." *Productivity Brief* (American Productivity Center), No. 33 (February 1984), pp. 1–6.

Tylczak, Lynn: "The Concept of Value Management: Creativity Creating Productivity." *Piedmont Airlines* (July 1985), pp. 51–53.

―――― : *White House Conference on Productivity Report.* Springfield, VA: National Technical Information Service, Department of Commerce, April 1984.

Woodruff, Marjorie: "Quality Circles: Wave of the Future or Fad?" *Resource* (November/December 1981), pp. 2–6.

Williams, Harry E.: "Quality + Productivity + Cost = Profit." *Quality Progress* (October 1984), pp. 17–20.

―――― : "Worker Participation Programs in Operation." *Productivity Improvement Programs* (The Bureau of National Affairs, Inc.), PPF Survey No. 138 (September 1984), pp. 13–16.

Yankelovich, Daniel, and John Immerwahr: "Putting the Work Ethic to Work." *Technology Review* (November/December 1983), pp. 13–17.

Index

A

Alstadt, Don 151
American Business Conference 128
American Productivity Center 7, 150
  "Camas, Washington Mill Reflects Crown Zellerbach's Renewed Attention to Human Resources" 164
  "Corning Glass Works Focuses on Quality Improvement" 165–166
  "Deming's Way" 66
  "Honeywell Aerospace and Defense Group" 7
  "National Semiconductor" 165
  Reward Systems and Productivity: A Final Report for the White House Conference on Productivity 87
  "ZEBCO, Inc." 162–164
American Society for Quality Control
  productivity of American workers 7–8
Anderson, Richard W. 127
AVCO Corporation 133, 161–162
  Cost of Quality 14, 127
  directive on quality 10–11
  Quality Quorums 161–162
AVCO Financial Services 56
AVCO Financial Services Canada 110, 166–168

B

Barrett, Will 166, 168
Bigbee, Carolyn J. 52
Bleemer, Judy 20–21
Bureau of National Affairs, Inc. 75

C

Celebration
  kickoff for Quality Has Value 94–95
  Quality Celebration 95–97
Certification of ideas 31, 59–60, 111–112
Charvat, John 162–163
Coca Cola 5
Collins, Frank C., Admiral (ret.) 54
Computers, use of
  Quality Team Tracking Program 26–31, 119–120
  Value Analysis 45
Corning Glass Works 165–166
Cost of nonconformance 99, 126–128
  definition 126
  graph 128
Cost of Quality 125–128
  categories 126
  definition 14
Crosby, Phillip B.
  definition of quality 4

Quality is Free 4, 12, 14, 20, 32, 126
Crown Zellerbach 164
Customer
  definition of 21–22, 167–168
  user-processor-supplier chain 22–23

D

Definitions for Quality Has Value
  Cost of Nonconformance 126
  Cost of Quality 14
  customer 21–22, 167–168
  process vs. program 26, 67
  quality 3–7
  Quality Ideas 101–104
  Quality Teams 61–62
  Value Analysis 37
Deming, Dr. W. Edwards
  customer 1
  quality and competition 8
  quality and management 8, 16, 66, 150
  statistical quality control 177
Departmental effort 8–10
Dewar, Donald L. 52, 56
Drucker, Peter F. 33

E

Ephlin, Donald 2
Essential purpose 39–40

F

Field force
  AVCO Financial Services/Canada 168
  certification of ideas 111–112
  "Field Force Quality Ideas" 118
  inception of Quality Has Value 110–112
  listening to 155–157
  Quality Field News 118
  recognition 112
  training 111–112
"Fred Retired" syndrome 145

Further Up The Organization 62–63

G

Gallup, Mr. 141, 153
Garvin, David A. 127
groupAction 26, 58–59, 63, 133, 168

H

Harris, Mr. 141, 153
Harvard Business Review 51, 52–53, 66–74
Harwood, Charles
  manager's apparent interest index 8
Hayes, Robert and Steven C. Wheelwright 173

I

IBM 127
  definitions for PRIDE Program 173
In Search of Excellence 32, 110, 152

J

Job security 2, 7, 35, 38, 130–131, 176–177
Juran, Dr. Joseph M.
  definition of quality 4
  statistical quality control 177
  user-processor-supplier 22

K

Kant, Mel 164
KISS 174
Kivenko, Ken
  quality and management 15–16
  quality and productivity 6

L

L.L. Bean 112
Langston, C.E. 20
Lantern 89, 100

Lawler, Edward E. III and Susan A. Mohrman 52, 66–74
Leadership, types of 141
Lodge, George C. and Bruce R. Scott 175
Luther, David 166

M

Management By Wandering Around (MBWA) 108–109, 152
Maritz Motivation Company 82
Maslow hierarchy of needs 78–81
  publicity 83–84
McDonald Aircraft Company 82
McGill, Arch 82
McKinsey and Company, Inc. 128
Megatrends 57
Miller, Lawrence 151
Mohrman, Susan A. and Edward E. Lawler III 52, 66–74
Most Valuable Player, Team 95–97, 99–100, 131

N

Naisbitt, John 18, 57
National Association of Suggestion Systems 88, 113, 137, 144
National Semiconductor 165
Nolan, Robert E. 25, 36
"Notes and Ideas" 117–118, 119

O

Obstacles to optimum value 38–39
Odiorne, George 19, 176
Olson, Val 16–18
"Our Policy Is Quality"
  letter 24
  slogan 13

P

PEET (Program for Ensuring Everybody's Thanked) 108–110, 152, 172, 178
Peterfreund, Stanley 149

Peters, Tom
  In Search of Excellence 32, 110
  statistical quality control 177
  skunkworks, first effort at The Paul Revere 8–10
  Toward Excellence 26
Pins 85–86, 98
  and Maslow's hierarchy of needs 89
  lunch-for-a-pin 89
Planning Review 128
PRIDE Program (IBM) 173
Process vs. Program 26, 67
Publications 178
  "Field Force Quality Ideas" 118
  "Notes and Ideas" 117–118, 119
  Quality Field News 118
  Quality News 89–90, 92–93, 96, 99, 100, 106–107, 116–118, 130
The Pursuit of Efficiency 58
Pym, Jeff
  three stages of quality process 162

Q

Quality
  AVCO directive 11
  AVCO Financial Services/Canada definition 167
  definition 3–7
  difference from productivity 6–7
  early definition 24
  job security 2, 7, 35, 38, 130–131, 176–177
Quality Celebration 95–97, 134
Quality Circle Institute 52
Quality Circles
  destructive forces 67–75
  problems with 52–54
  prototype for action 51–52, 54
  reasons for popularity 73
  relationship to Quality Teams 66
"Quality circles after the fad" 52, 66–74

Index

Quality Field News
  inception 118
  sample 118
Quality Has Value
  changes for 1985 131–132
  comparison of annual results 137
  components 16–17
  Cost of Quality definition and survey 14
  Field force 110–113
  inception 3, 16
  kickoff celebration 94–95
  objectives for 1985 99, 128–131
  results for 1984 (Home Office) 106–108, 125; (Field) 113
  results for 1985 (Home Office) 125, 136–137; (Field) 113
Quality ideas
  calculating savings 104–106, 112
  certification 31, 59–60, 100–106
  definition 101–104
Quality is Free 4, 12, 13, 14, 20, 32
Quality Month 1
Quality News 96, 99, 100, 106–107, 117–118, 130
  inception 89–90, 116–117
  sample 92–93
Quality Progress
Quality Quorums 161–162
Quality Steering Committee 12–15, 24
  composition of 12
  initial meetings 13
  meeting schedule change 32
  Quality Improvement Team 12, 24
Quality Team Central 27–31
Quality Team Tracking Program 26–31, 119–120, 135, 174
Quality Teams 174–175
  choosing Team Leaders 62–63
  composition 16, 55, 61–62
  matching authority and responsibility 20, 56–57, 60–61
  training Team Leaders 25–26, 57–60, 177

Quest (Quality Enhancement Strategy) 165

R

Reed, Willis 4
Reagan, Ronald 1
Recognition/gratitude/celebration 60, 178
  awards ceremonies 88
  certification of ideas 31, 59–60, 100–106
  cost 67
  Field force 112
  gifts, gift certificates 85, 88–90, 98–99, 112
  Maslow hierarchy of needs 78–81
  Most Valuable Player, Team 95–97, 99–100, 131
  pins 85–86, 89, 98
  publicity 83
  Quality News 89–90, 92–93
  variations 89, 91, 94
  standards 85, 87, 90, 112, 168
Reid, Aubrey K. 138–139
Results of Quality Has Value
  comparison 137
  QHV '84 106–108, 113, 125
  QHV '85 113, 125, 136–137
Rewards Systems and Productivity Final Report 87
Richards, Bob 52
Robert E. Nolan and Company 25, 34–36
Rogers, Richard G. 152

S

Sara Lee 5
Scott, Bruce R. and George C. Lodge 175
Shank, John 164
Statistical quality control 177
Suggestion System
  at The Paul Revere 27, 30, 95–96, 137

National Association of Suggestion Systems 88, 113, 137, 144
Surveys 121–123, 153–155
 AFS/Canada 166–167
 cost of nonconformance 99
 Cost of Quality 14
 "How'd We Do?" cards 121
 industry (attitude) 122, 154–155

T

Team Leaders
 groupAction 26
 Quality Has Value '85 63, 132–134
 training 25–26, 57–60, 177
Technology Review 57
Textron, Inc. 10, 54
Thorsteinson, Tim 165
Thurston, William R. 2
 definition of quality 6
Toward Excellence 26, 110
Townsend, Robert 62–63
Training
 Field force 111–113
 management 110, 114–116, 177
 new employees 113–114
 team leaders 25–26, 57–60, 177
Treybig, James G. 153
Tylczak, Lynn 34, 45–46, 49

V

Value Analysis
 and Quality Teams 15, 33, 44–45, 47, 133, 137, 174
 competing with quality—early efforts 11–12
 definition 37
 essential purpose 39–40
 examples of workshop results 47–48
 implementation of recommendations 123–124
 job security 35, 38
 participants 34–35, 37
 phases 36–49
 purpose 37
 results 47–48, 137
 Robert E. Nolan and Company 25, 34–36
Value Management 34, 49

W

Washington, Elsie 164
Wayne, John 142, 143
Wheaton, Warde
 quality and productivity 7
Wheelwright, Steven C. and Robert Hayes 173

Y

Yale Center for Creative Leadership 51
The Year Ahead 1986: Ten Powerful Trends Shaping Your Future 18

Z

ZEBCO, Inc. 162–164
Zenger-Miller, Inc. 25–26, 58, 168
 groupAction 26, 58–59, 63, 168
 Toward Excellence 26, 110
Zumwalt, Elmo, Admiral 159

There's an epidemic with 27 million victims. And no visible symptoms.

It's an epidemic of people who can't read.

Believe it or not, 27 million Americans are functionally illiterate, about one adult in five. Forty-seven million more are able to read on only the most minimal level. Together, that's almost 75 million Americans...one third of our entire population.

The solution to this problem is you...when you join the fight against illiteracy. So call the Coalition for Literacy at toll-free **1-800-228-8813** and volunteer.

Illiteracy may be an epidemic, but with a little caring from you, we can stop it.

**Volunteer Against Illiteracy.
The only degree you need
is a degree of caring.**

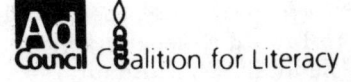

Ad Council   Coalition for Literacy